by Derek Wilson and Colin Newton

Published by Inclusive Solutions UK Limited

Published by Inclusive Solutions UK Ltd
January 2011
Images by Inclusive Solutions
Design by Cat Eglinton
Printed by Russell Printers
ISBN 0-9546351-6-7

Contents

Acknowledgements

We want to begin by thanking the many children and young people who we have had the privilege to meet, work with and hopefully further their experience of inclusion. You have taught us a lot.

We trace the inspiration and the root of many of the ideas developed in this book to the pioneering work of Inclusion Press in Toronto Canada, particularly the contributions of Jack Pearpoint and the late Marsha Forest. We will always owe them a debt of gratitude for inspiring and guiding the work of Inclusive Solutions and for stimulating our grasp and strengthening our realisation of the keys to inclusion.

We have also been deeply influenced by and owe enormous respect to the disabled people's movement across the UK - in particular the radical contributions made by Micheline Mason and Richard Rieser and more recently Tara Flood.

We would like to give particular thanks to Cat Eglinton for her key role in the design and layout of this book.

The Alliance for Inclusive Education and Disability Equality and Education have been extremely important in moving on the agenda for inclusive education. We all owe them.

We have been supported and influenced to by fellow professionals in the often-criticised world of educational psychology in which we have found individual champions for inclusion around the UK. You know who you are.

Thanks to those who have worked alongside us in the presentation of the *Keys* around the UK and beyond including Mole Chapman, Jackie Dearden, Ju Hayes, Micheline Mason, Jaynie Mitchell and Robin Tinker.

Thanks too to all those participants who have engaged with our training days so whole-heartedly. We have laughed and cried with you all in equal measure.

We acknowledge the many families across the UK that we have worked with and learned from - often in the middle of their battles for fair and equitable inclusive education.

Personally we could have done little without the love and support of our closest family. So thanks to Jacqui and Anne and also to the challenges, learning and encouragement offered by our sons and daughters – Cat and Jo, Elliot, Louis and Bethan.

Finally we need to recognise that we are only who we are because of who went before us. So we thank our parents for past and present love and direct support to us to this day.

Derek Wilson and Colin Newton
Nottingham 2010

Foreword by Micheline Mason

I have had the privilege of working alongside Derek And Colin as they take a roomful of strangers, brought together only by their 'job' and a hope to learn something useful on the subject of inclusion, on a journey full of emotional upheaval, new information, fun, tears and thoughtful re-evaluation of their past assumptions and knowledge. They do not teach so much about those 'others' who we seek to include, but about the commonness of our humanity and how we have failed to recognise it.

I am delighted therefore that this book is an attempt to sum up the insights embedded in their course called 'The Keys to Inclusion'. The reader is taken from the earliest beginnings – how do we make a person feel welcome? Why do some people not get the welcome they deserve? What is the history behind their experiences? You are led onwards into human services and their responses to people who do not fit the box of 'normality'. Drawn from their extensive experience as Educational Psychologists this section has much unique critical insight into some of the unnecessary barriers to learning faced by many children within the education system, and how those barriers can be removed. This will be of great interest to teachers and community educators, including parents.

Much of the rest of the book deals with the challenges of building inclusive communities in which we adults can live, love and work. This part of the story is to some degree futuristic, and about all of us – how we build sustainable futures for ourselves, our loved ones, our children and future generations. It is not so much a description of those communities, but an exploration of the values and the skills we all need to create something different.

As a physically disabled person who grew up in the deeply segregated 50's and 60's, I am very pleased to report that change is happening. Attitudes towards social class, race and ethnicity, sexual preference, age and disability are all becoming less judgemental, punitive and more enlightened. There is a growing desire for more than material prosperity, but for community, connection, purposefulness in life. We are drawing together to

protect the natural world and ultimately our own survival. But desire does not equal skill. This book is about how to start, profoundly practical and based in the messy reality of our ordinary lives, our fears and lack of knowledge. It is generous in its spirit, aiming to give back the power to the readers to start to 'be the difference they want to see'. A very hopeful act.

Introduction

This book is aimed at all who wish to work more inclusively with children, families, and communities. What are the keys that will ensure all can be present, participating and offering their best?

We have used our experience of working in schools and early years settings and all of our UK-wide training experience to inform this book.

This is a book about *inclusion* – a much used and misunderstood word. *Inclusion* has been a commonplace jargon word in the world of education and beyond over the last decade but what on earth does it mean? Every departmental vision statement and supporting principles will have the word *inclusion* in it somewhere. But it seems the word can be put to a wide range of uses. At one extreme, many segregated special schools are happy call themselves *inclusive* and many mainstream schools have created separate places within their buildings called *"Inclusion Units"*. At the other extreme is the thinking of Doug Biklen, Dean of Education at Syracuse University in New York State and a leading writer and researcher in inclusive education and disability studies. Biklen has been much more sparing over the past 25 years about where he thinks he has truly seen 'inclusion':

> **"The only place where full inclusion truly happens is in some families"**
> TASH Newsletter, Autumn 2001

So there is no obvious consensus out there on what is meant by the word 'inclusion'. This has not stopped the wholesale re-branding of local authority departments, support services and individuals' job titles. But we want to ask: what really changed in your work practices as a result of changing your name to *'The Inclusive Education Service'* or whatever? What did you stop doing? What did you start doing for the first time? If there are no obvious answers to these questions then it is fairly certain that this was a change of name only and no real understanding of inclusion was behind the re-branding.

We think the word inclusion has many meanings - all of them important - and in this book we call these meanings: *The Keys*. We will take a close look at 8 Keys to inclusion and the actions needed if these keys are to open up fresh possibilities and lead us into new places in our work.

The *Eight Keys to Inclusion* we will deal with in this book are:

1. **Welcome** – is about understanding how we create a sense of safety and a sense of belonging

2. **Learning to Listen** – is about noticing, asking and paying attention to what you hear

3. **The Long View** – is about understanding where we have come from as a society in the way we respond to those are different and is also about creating a vision of what a good life would look like in 20 or more years time for the young people we are working with today

4. **Painting Portraits – Not Testing Intelligence** – is about finding new ways of knowing people who are different or who challenge the status quo

5. **Learning** - *our* learning - is about recognising differences in styles, preferences and learning the accommodations and adjustments that support those differences

6. **The Intentional Building of Relationships** – is about creating places and ways of working together that build, maintain and repair the spaces between people

7. **Gifts** - is about recognising and nurturing contributions that everyone of us has to make

8. **Teams** – is about understanding that inclusion, done properly, is more than one person's work.

As we explore each of these Keys in turn we are interested in both the little things we can do differently tomorrow and in the shared vision we can create together of how our places could look years from now if we genuinely move towards a more inclusive future. It will help as you read this book, if you try and stay as open-minded as you can. What might we be able to achieve to make these keys a real part of the places we live and work?

The First Key: Welcome

> "Inclusion means all students educated as full-time, valued, and participating members of their age appropriate general education classes in their neighbourhood and schools, AND the supports provided to students, teachers, and families so all can be successful."
> Autism National Community, 2002.

In the beginning was the welcome...

Without welcome you do not properly enter, you are not present and so do not participate or perform. 'WELCOME' is the first key to successful inclusion.

Everyone who needs a relationship needs a welcome. Particular efforts need to be made when welcoming parents, carers, pupils and other family members into any situation which is unfamiliar to them or in which they are likely to feel anxious, apprehensive, aggressive or defensive. This is often the case for people invited to our meetings, reviews and case conferences.

"Welcome: to receive with gladness, to admit willingly"
The Chambers Dictionary 9th Edition

The UK Audit Commission asked Parent Partnership Officers around the country which families had problems gaining admission to their local schools.

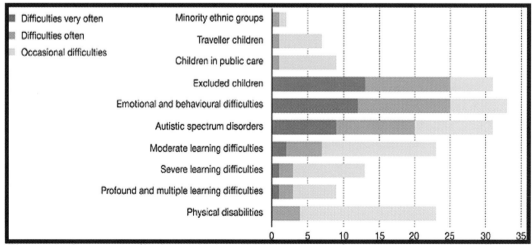

Figure 1: Source Audit Commission (2002) survey of parent partnership officers

Their findings said that pupils who had been excluded, those with behaviour-related labels and anyone with autism all had problems with securing a school place in the usual ways – a problem with being welcomed. It appears that some children and their families get much less of a welcome than others.

Of course the welcome extended to some of us in a whole range of community settings will be different depending on who we are judged to be. Differences in apparent sexuality, race, culture, social class, perceived impairments, behaviour, physical appearance and reputation can all dramatically affect how an individual is welcomed.

> **"Many have reported that school environments driven by league tables, targets and inspection cycles have often made certain pupils less welcome when it is judged that such prospective pupils may reduce the performance of a school."**
> SEN Select Committee, 2006

If we want to make our welcome more inclusive then we would do well to start with the physical symbols and environment in which the welcome takes place.

Symbols of Welcome

- Light, warmth, and soft, rather than harsh, furnishings – pot plants and flowers

- Waiting area with a settee to sit on and a cup of tea offered on arrival

- Toys and books suitable for a range of different children and young people

- Pictures and posters reflecting the cultures and differences present in the local community

- Soothing music

Offers of drinks and even food are clear welcome messages, both profound and often cultural in their importance. How do you welcome someone to your own home?

In larger groups the welcome given in situations such as training events, conferences, parents evenings, and other gatherings will benefit from food, drink, sweets, music and colour as they all provide tangible symbols of welcome.

"Its about making sure people are heard and feel part of what's going on. It's about not having a norm which is supposed to be performed"
Maresa Mackeith, 2009

Smiles, tone of voice, warm words, handshakes, and even hugs are a great form of welcome without words. The physicality of the welcome depends on your relationship with the person and their cultural and personal preferences and expectations. Some enjoy a firm handshake, others a hug, whilst others need plenty of space. Keep it respectful.

In larger gatherings, the welcome needs more stage management and can be bigger and more dramatic. Open body posture and upturned hands can accompany effusive, warm welcomes. This is not a time to hold back or to only pick out certain people for a welcome.

Creating a sense of Safety & Belonging

Through dialogue and consensus building, ground rules or shared promises can develop. This in turn creates a structure and routine essential for a sense of safety and belonging; this is crucial for setting the right tone for any gathering or meeting.

Self-revelation, openness and sincerity from those welcoming a group or individual of any age or background can help enormously with building a sense of safety and trust.

"Love is to protect and border and to greet each other"
Rainer Maria Rilke

Providing choices and opt out possibilities for what may be perceived as risky activities, can be reassuring for the anxious, eg "It is ok to say 'pass'."

What Else Helps?

- Be clear

- Acknowledge real challenges

- Use humour to relax and strengthen a group

- Be honest and respectful.

Safety, particularly for our children and vulnerable adults, has never been more important. How can we make sure that school, settings and other places in which we work in communities are as safe as possible? Criminal Record checks will only take us so far, become out of date as soon they are created - but give a misleading sense of safety.

"We have a policy that, with the little kids, at least 2 adults/care providers are present so that there is an accountability/protective structure. With the youth – yes - pairs or threes to assure the same.

Reality is that people get hurt in spite of protective measures, in all kinds of situations. We opt not to do "background checks" because they are not a community structure of protection, they are an institutional "solution." And if they truly worked we would not be seeing so much abuse in foster and institutionalized care where background checks are required. So we opt for a community/relational approach.

It is also our experience that even people with a history of "challenging behaviors" behave better in a circle of community.

Good news also to knowledge we have not had an abuse incident in our 12 years of building community."
Lois Smidt, 2009, Beyond Welfare

Ensuring more than one person is always present with another is one of the more practical ways of dealing with the challenging issue of safety. No one should ever be left on their own with a person unknown to them. We continue to think together and debate this issue.

Physical contact, including hugs, is essential for many children and adults to feel connected emotionally. There has been so much caution around this issue in the UK and elsewhere that many practitioners are virtually forbidden to touch the children they work with in any way at all. We seem to have forgotten that abuse is by nature secretive and occurs mostly in the family home and in our separate 'special' institutions. Have we gone too far in our caution in our ordinary community settings? Many would say we have. We heard this comment while preparing this book:

"I did not think I should tie her hair up for her"
Teaching Assistant, Primary School, Lancashire

It must be time to re-evaluate our approach to touch physical contact and allow common sense to return. Touch is crucial to establishing a sense of belonging and ultimately to the healthy social and emotional development of human beings.

Lose the Magnifying Glass

In our western culture we have a strong tendency to be very self-critical as well as judgemental of each other. In schools everyone is judged, tested, assessed!

We magnify each other's faults and our own. We start with physical difference then move quickly to how people act, behave, what they say and how they say it! We look at ourselves in the mirror, real or imagined and the critical observations begin: *look at that nose, how fat you are!....* and so on.

Then our negative inner voices can get hold: *you are not good enough, clever enough, quick enough...* and the old favourite: *'One day, despite my fancy title, my professional front, they are going to find me out...its just little old me and I don't know much!'*

In our work, we encourage people to put their magnifying glasses aside and try and keep them away the length of the time we are together.

Alternatively using a judge's wig as a prop and then dramatically removing it, as inspired by Jack Pearpoint, (Inclusion Press, Toronto, Canada) is a simple way of reminding each other that it will help if we are not critical of the session leaders, each other or ourselves.

We have found that when we playfully talk about the serious subjects of judgement and the magnification of mistakes, we can create a safer climate. When we achieve this, children and adults will always become more communicative and creative. They will try out ideas, play and take risks and learning will be optimised.

Communicating without Jargon

We find use of the *Jargon Buster* or *'Crap Detector'* to be an essential part of our training sessions. Jack Pearpoint and Marsha Forest from Inclusion Press, Toronto taught us the power of this prop. This instrument is rattled when anyone in the room uses jargon, strange abbreviations or hard to understand sentences. Our teaching has improved since the rattle has sounded in our ears! If something is worth saying it can be said plainly. Too many parents and others are sitting in review meetings right at this minute with only faintest idea what the professionals are talking about and they go away feeling stupid. Jargon excludes people and we need to invent props or

processes that make it unacceptable. We commend the use of the jargon-buster in any review meeting where parents and pupils may be present. Who should get to hold the *buster*? We think you know the answer...everyone!

Or, how about following the lead of the People First movement in the UK who recommend holding up a card with a question mark on it when something is not understood in a meeting.

The *jargon buster* has a role in any learning situation. Try it out in adult training venues as well as classrooms. The risk of appearing foolish may seem high but the promises of greater understanding and increased participation are there for all.

Rituals & Routines

For many children, young people and adults, the use of welcoming rituals and routines can be empowering and provide a heightened sense of security. This is especially important for pupils living in unpredictable family situations, surviving neglect, abuse or loss. It is just as important for those whose impairments lead to a greater feeling of anxiety than others.

Rituals and routines may simply relate to what happens at the start of a day, start of lessons and other key transition points. From standing behind chairs, queuing in corridors, chanting responses, to prayers; all have their value and place in ordered welcome, if this is *what-we-do-round-here*.

A good welcome should be effectively managed and never left to chance.

Inclusion and the Welcome

If we can successfully welcome disabled or challenging children and young people to our settings - we set the tone for all that will follow. Communities, schools and families that embrace inclusion are so often the most welcoming to all who participate or visit them.

Jonathon was joining a new secondary school. He was 13 and carried the label of autism. His welcome needed to be carefully considered as new people and places were likely to make him very anxious. What was put in place really helped him to make a great start at his new school. The elements of a good welcome Jonathon were:

- Being able visit the new school at a time when there was no one else there

- Looking at photos of key staff and pupils he would meet

- Watching a video of the school in action, showing breaks, lunchtimes and various subjects being taught in different rooms around the school

- Being given a map of the school

- Setting up a meeting between his tutor group and his parents in which information about Jonathon's differences, strengths and interests was established. The pupils in his tutor group were then able to ask questions respectfully.

- Using the school's progressive model of cooperation, grouping pupils by interests and skills rather than ability, wherever possible

- Being met by a small welcoming committee of other pupils who knew the school well and who became a supportive circle of friends, meeting weekly for his first year at the school

- Allowing a support assistant from his previous school to work with Jonathon for the first 3 weeks at his new school

Practical Implications

There are many ways we can improve the welcome we offer:

- Spend a day together with your team, group or family reflecting on the quality of the welcome in your setting. Who takes responsibility for welcome? Who is at the front door? What rituals and symbols are present already, which could be added?

- Consider those who are least likely to be welcomed in your setting. What could be done to improve the welcome for them? What would make them feel safe or a sense of belonging?

Inclusive Solutions

- What will you do about jargon in your setting?

- Who can go ahead to be there to build the bridge for the person you know will struggle to feel welcome? What could they do to prepare people and to make the situation feel as welcoming as possible?

- How will you ensure a sense of safety and belonging for all?

- Turn up the volume on the quality of your own welcome up by 80%. What impact does this have on your life and work?

> **'Each one of us needs**
>
> **In order to be included,**
>
> **To live a life amongst people**
>
> **Who can embrace our differences**
>
> **And in so doing**
>
> **Embrace their own.**
>
> **Don't make us normal**
>
> **Make us welcome'**
>
> From: *'The Spa School Blues'* – a poem written by Micheline Mason (Mason 2006) after watching 'Make Me Normal' a Channel 4 television documentary (June 2005) featuring four young people with autism who all attend a large state-run special school.

Hard Questions

- How do we welcome parents who we know are abusers?
- How do we keep community safe without destroying trust?
- How do we welcome child sex offenders into a community?
- How do we welcome children who are so extreme in their behaviour that they are very likely to hurt more vulnerable children?

Resources

- Antwone Fisher. Film – View the scene where Antwone a violent, confused young man badly abused as a child is welcomed back into his extended family that he has never met = A five star welcome.

The Second Key: Learning to Listen

> "It's about time and taking time to really absorb what's happening. We can't listen to each other without space and time so those things have to be built into a timetable."
>
> Maresa Mackeith, 2009

Who needs to be listened to? Surely we ALL do?

Some parents tell us their child was welcomed to the school or setting but when it got hard the staff stopped listening. Have you ever been told negative things about your child and their behaviour? How did it feel? Do you know parents who have had this experience? What do you notice about the emotional experience of being told but not listened to?

Many children and young people let us know only too clearly:

 **'No one listens to me!'**

The older they get the louder this message! Even young people with no spoken words can still let us know when they do not feel listened to. Herb Lovett (1996) a psychologist from the United States, was clear that we should take people seriously. He thought that their actions and words are communications and may carry meanings that are not always obvious unless we listen very closely. Herb's work was with adults with challenging behaviour and locked away in residential settings. Towards the end of his life he wrote a book called: *Learning to Listen*. You'll notice that his book was not called, *Rewards-and-Punishments-for-Hard-to-Manage-Adults*.

Consider the 4 year old who loudly shouts out:

 **F... off!**

These two simple words can mean so many things if we listened carefully.

"Leave me alone. I am extremely angry. No one is listening to me. Help."

The 12-year-old who rips the display work off the walls of his classroom may be communicating a range of possible meanings. We need to listen carefully to words and actions. We can listen to behaviour if we try hard enough.

"I am very upset. My work is useless. I am jealous of the work that is being presented. Look at me now. Help."

We have found that when working around an individual in groups of all sizes or working as a diverse group trying to achieve consensus, listening will always be key. Listening activities designed to deepen listening can help set a tone but also strengthen the connections between those present. Starting with the simplest activities of listening uninterrupted for one minute, to activities designed to encourage deeper listening skills of reflecting back, summarising and use of open-ended questions.

The purposes of empathic listening whilst making use of reflecting back and paraphrasing include:

- An indication of real listening: 'You have heard what I am saying because you have repeated it.' Many therapists have argued that to be really listened to like this can actually bring about personal growth and change with no other intervention being present.
- Clearly noticing and amplifying key words and phrases.
- Gaining process time by slowing up. When a facilitator reflects back during person centred planning, time is gained and a repeat of the contribution is made for a graphic facilitator to hear better and translate into key words or graphics on a wall chart.
- Such processes to help whoever is present to hear and reflect upon what has just been said.

Having reflected back we have also found it helpful to check out with the speaker, 'have I got it right?' and 'was that it?' especially when paraphrasing a long input. If the speaker has spoken at length you will inevitably need to paraphrase what you have heard. However it is essential to respectfully stay with the person's own words and not substitute your own. By 'psychologising' other people's words with your own, you will only create distance and break the connection that is being made with the speaker.

Some are not comfortable with intense listening and this needs to be respected. They do not like being under a spotlight and may easily feel judged by an empathic listener.

During person-centred processes, such as the MAP or PATH processes, (Pearpoint, J. Forest, M. and Snow, J., 1993) it is essential to emphasise the importance of respectful listening. Listening is also crucial for all practitioners who are working with people of all ages especially when tackling issues involving challenging behaviour in more restorative ways. Tinker (2008) puts it this way:

"The various processes that can be used to repair harm demand certain skills of facilitators. These include active, empathic listening, impartiality and an ability to empower others to come up with their own solutions to problems."
Newton and Mahaffey, 2008

Great listening often delivers empathy, which in its own right can improve relationships, deepen understanding and promote healthy behaviour change.

"I notice that empathy is a key ingredient in any successful restorative conference. When the parties learn about the weaknesses and humanness of those who have previously been offenders, opponents or competitors, there is often a kind of catharsis. People can forgive a lot, when they understand how something came to happen."
Drewery, 2008

Listening deeper, under the surface of words, is where the true meaning lies. Listening to the story, the narrative - has a power of its own

"All of those people trying so hard to help me. All of them hoping for me to do well, all wanting to be kind and useful, all feeling how important helping me was. Yet never did anyone one of them ask me what it was like for me. They never asked me what I wanted for myself. They never asked me if I wanted their help. I do not feel entirely grateful. I feel, instead, a remote anger stored beneath my coping pattern of complacent understanding. People do the best they can to help in meaningful ways, I know. I just wish all the disabled children would say to their helpers: Before you do anything else, just listen to me."
Marsha Saxton, 1985

Inclusive
Solutions

Offering a speaker something to hold when addressing a group can have ritual importance and amplify listening in a room. Aboriginal talking sticks or precious stones can be held by a speaker to elevate the gravity of their presence and clarify who actually is speaking. We like to use magic wands that light up!!

Listening appears such a simple and familiar process and yet we need a lifetime to figure it out. Many teachers and other practitioners working with children and young people and those working with disabled and other marginalised groups, whilst recognising the rhetoric of listening to people, regularly fail to do so.

> **"We all have the power to listen to voices that are seldom heard. If we choose to make the time, to learn to listen and to struggle with the pain and frustration that disempowered people feel, we will see new visions, feel new energy, and find hope in our future. There is power in the powerless. We can be catalysts, or encrusted residue. The choice is ours."**
> Pearpoint 1993

Practical Implications

- Practice listening with someone you trust. Try and use as few words as possible. Invite feedback.
- Next time you are listening to someone as part of your work try reflecting back facts and feelings.
- Identify someone who does not use words to communicate and work and really listen to them. Notice what you learn.

Hard Questions

- What do you do when you're listening to views radically different to your own?
- How do you/should you even listen to someone talking in abusive terms about another person?
- What do you do if you have developed habits that are not conducive to good listening?

Resources

- Listening Sticks, flashing magic wands
- Videos that stimulate thinking about inclusion- such as Including Samuel – see www.includingsamuel.com for a summary preview of this documentary.

The Third Key: The Long View

> "I see a society that needs change and I think the change needs to be in how we care about each other and about making vulnerability an important aspect of us all or to focus on. So people can be vulnerable without feeling it's a weakness. Then the whole of society could cooperate rather than always be in competition."
> Maresa Mackeith, 2009

We so often take a very short-sighted view when planning for the education of very challenging or disabled children. What is happening today, this week, this term or at best this year is the dominant preoccupation in the UK education system and elsewhere.

"Darren has head butted the Teaching Assistant...this has gone on too long already; he has to go...."

Such an incident can preoccupy professionals when they sit down to plan for meeting Darren's educational needs. Yet a decision to change school placement will affect his whole life as well as that of the community in which he is a member.

What do you want to be when you grow up?
How often have you heard this question asked of typical children? What was your own answer as a child to this question?

However, so often we will not ask this same question of disabled children and families will often say 'we dare not think beyond today' let alone into the long term future. So we go about planning for children with complex impairments as if they did not really have a long-term future and adulthood. We make major decisions such as placement in a special school or unit without having regard for the long-term implications of such a move. When that child becomes an adult they are at great risk of being isolated from the wider community. They may even be very vulnerable within the wider community or they may find they are completely excluded from it. We live in a society that does not have special shops or special bus stops....

Yet when we really take the long view backwards as well as forwards we can be truly amazed and can learn much to inform our planning. Let's start by looking back...

Colin with Nanny Warren & Sister Jane, 1959

A special person...

This is Colin's mum's mum, his maternal grandmother, known as Nanny Warren. This wonderful lady was passionate about life, loved singing, playing the piano and photography. At 16 she played piano at the Crystal Palace in London with a full orchestra. She played piano for the local *Co op Juniors* for many years. For most of the years Colin knew her she was largely housebound. When visiting Nanny Warren you would be regaled with stories of the war, of past musical concerts and people she had known. Deep into Colin's adolescence and then on into his early 20s, he would visit his beloved Nanny Warren. He would then be required to sing *Amazing Grace* at the old piano before departing. What drew Colin perhaps even more powerfully than all of this was Nanny Warren's gift of being able to communicate something extraordinary over the space between the two of them: unconditional acceptance and love.

This unconditional acceptance was communicated largely non-verbally through the twinkle of an eye; a special smile a connection they both knew was present. Words to spell this out were few. Possibly the phrase: 'you lovely boy', might punctuate what was achieved mostly silently. No special programme was needed between them to boost Colin's self-esteem, just unconditional love and acceptance readily received.

In fact the essential ingredients for inclusion were present in this relationship. Nanny gave Colin all he needed to be truly present; complete acceptance, love and someone who would always listen. Colin belonged.

Nanny Warren has been dead some 30 years, but of course she is alive in Colin's heart, mind and soul. Part of her lives through him as it always does when we are well included by someone, their gift flows through us; it stays with us and others benefit later. What a message of hope. We can do this today for someone. You could already be doing this without realising.

You may not have a Nanny Warren in your life, but no matter how painful, shadowy or dark your life has been so far, you will have known someone who stepped forward from the shadows and was there for you. Someone who believed in you, reached out to you, helped you at a crucial point in your life or simply opened a door. **Remember them**. What was it about the relationship that made them so special? What did they bring? They may have been a teacher, parent, brother, friend, community person, or even a partner in more recent years. Recall them. What did they give you?

Reflect on people in your own life then ask others. This is a key question, who do you remember who was there for you? What was it about the relationship that worked so well? These are the ingredients for inclusion. Here lies all the information we need to create more inclusive families, schools and communities. We have listened to hundreds of these amazingly magical stories over the years and are constantly moved by the simplicity and wonder of inclusive relationships.
Just being there... accepting me for who I was whatever I did... encouraging... unconditional support... wanted more for me...saw something special in me... treated me as if I was part of their family...opened the door to their culture...made a special effort for me...The words go on.

These stories of love and connection help us understand the importance of taking the long view - just as people are there in our past, here we are for others in the present.

Some people like to haunt themselves with the question: what is the worst disability?

We have no doubt that it is loneliness. That is the enemy.

We have one disabled friend who names indifference as even more chilling. Others will reach for incarceration, or isolated imprisonment as even worst ways to end up.

As you read this you will know of children that are pushing the system, that are very likely to be excluded or segregated. What you do in that child's life can make all the difference to whether they exist within a network of fulfilling relationships or whether they become isolated adults. Anything you can do to hold that young person within their mainstream community will help maximise their opportunities for longer term, fulfilling relationships.

So this is where we return to the child who is hard to include and decisions we take about them now. Imagine you are a child at school with a boy called Aaron. We decide that Aaron is too difficult. He is aggressive, he keeps strangling Linda, and he keeps having tantrums, thrashing around on the floor. He barely uses any expressive language and does not seem to be learning much. What to do? Is he just too hard to include?

We can go two ways....

We can decide that he is too hard to include. Let us send him off to a unit or special school.
We can decide that we will hang on to Aaron. We will work on understanding his behaviour and his relationship with Linda and others. Some days it will not be easy. We will include him.

When we roll the clock forward into the long view we see the full implications for our early decisions.

There we are on a bus 20 years on... we see a large man throw himself onto the floor and begin thrashing around. Who is he? He seems weird and dangerous. Surely the worst excesses of a care in the community policy done on the cheap...this man should not be out on his own. No one knows him.

Consider the same scenario, but this time you know him; it's Aaron, surely? You stand and lean over him: *Aaron have you still got that cat?* The man leaps to his feet with a smile on his face. You know him. No, he still does not have much language, but he still loves cats and he recognises your voice.

The prizes of inclusion over the long term are great and varied. Maybe many more people will recognise Aaron's face and quite a few will know his name. A number may have learned of his interests

and his gifts. A few may have active relationships going on with him still. He may have friends; he may even have a partner.

David Quinton's (1987) study: *The Consequences of Care: Adult Outcomes from Institutional Rearing* followed a group of girls brought up in residential care and interviewed them over a decade later to assess the quality and stability of their lives as young adults. Some had achieved relatively settled, secure lives, others were still struggling and their lives were messy and chaotic with many failed relationships and bad decisions. Within the group of young women who were doing relatively well almost all recalled someone who had made a huge difference to them in their lives. They remembered someone who had expressed a belief in them, had seen and expressed the best in them and enabled them to believe they could be somebody. The person was often a teacher. What was particularly interesting was that when the researchers tracked back there was no indication that the person was having any obvious effect on the girl's behaviour *at the time.* It was only years later that the full impact of the relationship emerged.

This is encouragement to take the long view however challenging the pupils that we are working with may be. Often we will need to run the clock forward 10 years or more to fully appreciate the outcomes of our efforts with young people. Just holding in there, keeping the faith, believing in the possibility of change and in the value of the person, simply bearing witness or connecting in one of the amazing ways we explored earlier is likely be hugely beneficial to the child involved – though we ourselves may never get to see this.

A Sense of Belonging

Boys Brigade Camp 1969

For Colin, growing up and feeling included was made more solid by experiences of belonging to groups in the local community. Such groups included the local Boys Brigade. Some of his oldest friendships were made in this organisation. The annual camping experience was a particularly powerful time for community bonding and friendship development.

The ingredients were simple. A week spent together living on a field in tents. Groups of young people shared a tent and were expected to work together as a team, facing the challenges of tent inspections, sports and of course living communally. There was a lot of laughter, spiritual reflections, and rituals and routines culminating in a camp concert in which all engaged.

When Colin left home he continued to seek out such experiences of belonging, challenge and enjoyment. This led him to join brass bands placed local to the university or college he was currently attending. Below is a picture of the first brass band he enjoyed attending away from his home town. He will always look for opportunities to join and to participate in community throughout his life. Can you see how his long view experiences have led to this?

Morecambe and Heysham Silver band 1976 (spot bearded Colin 3 in on back row)

Practical Implications

How can we incorporate the long view into our regular daily practices? If you wish to go further in order to ground the idea of the long view, what can you do? Well - it is possible to build long view questions into planning from the early years onwards. Some key questions are well caught by John O'Brien in his essay: *Great Questions and The Art of Portraiture* (Inclusion News 2002) Try asking:

- *Who will need to know John and what kind of experience will they need to have with each other so that someone in our circle will offer John employment when he leaves school?*

- *What do we need to be doing together over the next ten years for this to happen?*

We may be asking these questions of a child who is as young as three years or younger; the long view will influence the answers.

Another valuable resource for long view thinking is Al Etmanski's book: *A Good Life.* This is the premier publication from the Canadian advocacy organisation: PLAN (Planned Lifetime Advocacy Network). Their aim is to support families of disabled young people to regain control of the simple, fundamental questions:

- *What do we want?*
- *What is a good life?*

The book is dedicated to showing families and their supporters how to plan effectively for the best outcomes that can be imagined for a young person.

All of the tools that come under the heading of *Person-Centred Planning* (e.g. MAPS, PATH, Essential Lifestyle Planning) are premised on the planning team having given serious thought to long view outcomes first. Become more familiar with these tools as ways of increasing your capacity to take the long view. They nearly all begin with a wonderful and ultimate long view question:

- *What is your dream?*
- Some also include questions around 'the story so far' and the 'nightmare' for the future. Such questions are not only therapeutic they also flush out deepest thoughts, values and inspiration as well as darkest concerns and unvoiced worries.

We should also use the wonderful question that Herb Lovett (1996) saved up for those really complex case conferences, where all kinds of professionals gather around an individual's challenging behaviour. He would ask: "Who loves this person?"

Whatever the reply, Herb's advice was that this was where you should begin... In the context of the long view the implications are even more obvious. We may need to radically reach out to the unsung heroes of family and community life who quietly hold the capacity to provide love and friendship in abundance if invited.

We will know when we have really worked on getting the long view right when in our work we can confidently ask disabled children and those with challenging behaviour:

What do you want to be when you grow up?

Hard Questions

- What do we do when no one knows a person's story?
- How can we challenge a parent who refuses to look beyond today?
- How can we hold the long view for a child who is dying?

Resources

- Old family video as stimulus for long view thinking
- Archived video of institutional life e.g. Stolen Lives (BBC production)
- PATH and MAP workbooks and video/DVD material from Inclusion Press
- Al Etmanski's book: *A Good Life.* This is the premier publication from the Canadian advocacy organisation: PLAN (Planned Lifetime Advocacy Network).

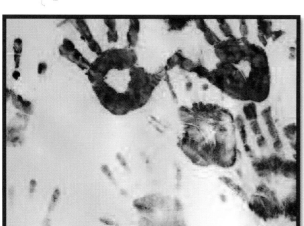

The Fourth Key: Paint Portraits – Don't Test Intelligence

'I think it is about seeing a contribution to the whole, even if a person does nothing his presence and the care he engenders is a contribution to the whole. It changes the atmosphere to a place where everyone can care for each other'.
Maresa Mackeith, 2009

For disabled people or those who have struggles with their learning and communication the focus on *what is missing* in them is nowhere more dramatically demonstrated than in considerations of *intelligence*. When diagnosing a child's learning difficulties, the IQ test and other forms of psychometric assessment continue to be widely and regularly used across the UK, Europe, the US and elsewhere as a way of 'measuring' the hypothetical concept known as 'intelligence'. Test scores arrived at from this process continue to be a key factor decision-making around school placements.

"We have to provide an IQ score so that the child and Adolescent Mental Health Team can allocate their resources. They keep asking us...."
Principal Educational Psychologist, 2008, Unnamed UK Local Authority

It is sad that what follows still needs to be written in 2010! – but perhaps we all need a sharp reminder of just what we put in jeopardy when we think we can summarise a person's capacity and worth with a test score number...

The Story So Far

Intelligence testing began in earnest in 1904 in France, when to find a method to differentiate between children who were 'intellectually normal' and those who were 'inferior'. The purpose was to put the latter into special schools where they would receive more individual attention. In this way the disruption they caused in the education of intellectually normal children could be avoided. Sound a familiar rationale?

Such thinking was a natural development from Darwinism and also Sir Francis Galton's Eugenics movement which dated back to 1869. Galton, a famous scientific polymath, promoted the idea that for society to prosper the 'weakest' should not be allowed to reproduce as this would adversely affect the genetic stock of future generations. Galton and his many followers, were contemptuous of any impact education might have on raising the achievement of the 'least able' (Thomas and Loxley, 2007).

What is Eugenics?

Eugenics is the study and practice of selective breeding applied to humans, with the aim of improving the species. In a historical and broader sense, eugenics can also be a study of "improving human genetic qualities." Advocates of eugenics sought to counter what they regarded as dysgenic dynamics within the human gene pool, specifically in regard to congenital disorders and factors relating to the heritability of IQ.

Widely popular in the early decades of the 20th century, it has largely fallen into disrepute after having become associated with Nazi Germany.

Galton, born in Birmingham in the UK, invented the term eugenics in 1883 and set down many of his observations and conclusions in a book, *Inquiries into human faculty and its development*. He believed that a scheme of 'marks' for family merit should be defined, and early marriage between families of high rank be encouraged by provision of monetary incentives. He pointed out some of the tendencies in British society, such as the late marriages of eminent people, and the paucity of their children, which he thought were dysgenic. He advocated encouraging eugenic marriages by supplying able couples with incentives to have children.

Francis Galton

Binet's work led to the development of the *Binet Scale,* also known as the *Simon-Binet Scale* in recognition of Theophile Simon's assistance in its development. It constituted a revolutionary

approach to the assessment of individual mental ability. However, Binet himself cautioned against misuse of the scale or misunderstanding of its implications. According to Binet, the scale was designed with a single purpose in mind; it was to serve as a guide to identify children in schools who required special education. Its intention was not to be used as 'a general device for ranking all pupils according to mental worth'. Binet also noted that:

> **"The scale, properly speaking, does not permit the measure of intelligence, because intellectual qualities are not superposable and therefore cannot be measured as linear surfaces are measured."**

The notion of an 'Intelligence Quotient' (IQ) was first developed by Terman in The United States in 1916. However, according to Binet, intelligence could not be described by a single score. Therefore the use of IQ as a definitive statement of a child's intellectual capability would be a serious mistake. In addition, Binet feared that IQ measurement would be used to condemn a child to a permanent 'condition' of stupidity, thereby negatively affecting his or her education and livelihood:

> **"Some recent thinkers...[have affirmed] that an individual's intelligence is a fixed quantity, a quantity that cannot be increased. We must protest and react against this brutal pessimism; we must try to demonstrate that it is founded on nothing."**

Binet's scale had a profound impact on educational development in the UK, the United States and elsewhere. However, the American and UK educators and psychologists who championed and utilised the scale and its revisions failed to heed Binet's caveats. Soon intelligence testing assumed an importance and respectability far out of proportion to its actual value.

When Cyril Burt was appointed as the first educational psychologist for London in 1913 he was much less cautious than Binet when it came to applying mental quotients. A Social Darwinist, he was enthusiastic about and deeply convinced of the genetic basis of intelligence. This gave great stimulus and a spurious objectivity to the move towards a segregated education system based on categorisation of children.

> **"Belief in the importance of intelligence and in the tests that purportedly measured it gave rise to a selective and segregative education system, following the high profile work of some influential educational psychologists. ... And this kind of thought is still revered especially in considering children's failure at school."**
> Thomas and Loxley, 2007

Burt's reputation is now linked to his fraudulent invention of data about inherited intelligence based on non-existent twin studies but at the time his influence was enormous. When medical officers in the UK were mainly responsible for determining pupils' educational difficulties and school placements, the single most important tool in their assessment was the Stanford-Binet Intelligence Scale.

Psychometric tools are still being used by significant numbers of educational psychologists across the UK. These tools have been revised and updated and typically include tests such as the WISC-R and the BAS (British Ability Scales) – the names may have changed a little but their purposes and core constructs remain unaltered.

This is surprising as the shortcomings of such tools have been long known and debated among educational psychologists in the educational establishment and beyond. Yet normative scores and test results still carry significant weight in how resources are allocated by local authorities and what school placements are deemed necessary to meet need. The IQ score remains one answer to the medical model question *"What's wrong with this child"*. There is a wealth of literature that is critical of the role and negative impact of IQ testing (Leyden, 1978, Lokke et. al, 1997; Leadbetter, 2005, Farrell and Venables, 2008) and yet educational psychologists still spend the bulk of their time undertaking formal special education evaluations using psychometric assessment including IQ tests (Shapiro et al., 2004 and Farrell and Venables, 2009).

> **"For some thirty years a few clear sighted professionals have been telling us that normal, abnormal, retarded, autistic, etc., are political, social, cultural notions rather than reflections of some objective, clearly discernible reality. They have been saying that like intelligence, mental retardation is not a 'thing' at all."**
> Anne Donnellan and Martha Leary, 1994

Why are IQ and other forms of psychometric assessment so inappropriate for understanding the learning and support needs of disabled children? Why is this so problematic?

Test scores are appealing in the messy and complex world of children's learning and in the demanding and oppressive world in which many contemporary educational professionals find themselves. They offer the immediate and seductive appeal of a seemingly precise, defined judgement of a child or young person, satisfying to the assessor but, as we shall see, yielding virtually no useful information about the child.

"We pass through this world but once. Few tragedies can be more extensive than the stunting of life, few injustices deeper than the denial of an opportunity to strive or even to hope, by a limit imposed from without, but falsely indentified as lying within."
Steven Gould 'The Mismeasure of Man' (1996)

Cultural Bias

Psychometric tests, as devised and used in the UK and the United States, were primarily developed by being tried out on white, middle-class children. This is how a view on what was a 'normal' score was reached. These tests are therefore likely to be both unfair and invalid when used on children from different cultural backgrounds. Researchers became aware of the problem that tests were in fact culturally derived and represented the ideas, attitudes and the linguistic concepts of the people who developed them. Attempts to create tests that are culturally neutral have proved unsuccessful, and there has not been any way found to develop a test that does not penalise some cultural groups while rewarding others.

The tests have been challenged in court for being racially and culturally biased, but there have been no definitive rulings on them. In the U.S. California law case, *Larry P. vs. Riles (1978)*, the court ruled that use of the tests was discriminatory, but two years later in an Illinois case, Pase *vs.* Hannon, it was decided that the tests were not culturally biased and could be used to place children in special education courses.

The concern over cultural bias raised a related issue among critics: *what is actually measured by the tests*? The critics assert that mental abilities and potential are gauged by simply adding up correct answers. This procedure necessarily ignores how a child has arrived at the answers hence the tests only measure the products of intelligence, without considering the processes by which the intelligence works. Critics assert that this means wrong answers would indicate a lower intelligence and a lessened potential; but research has demonstrated that the child who comes up with a wrong answer may understand as much about a problem as the one who gives the correct answer, perhaps by guessing. Furthermore, the complexity of skills and intelligence may be as great in a different cultural group, but test questions may need to be approached in another way because of differences in cultural background.

> **"Cultures differ with respect to the importance they place on competition with peers in performing tasks or solving problems, on speed or quality of performance, and on variety of other test-related behaviors. Some cultures emphasize concrete rather than abstract problem solving, often to the extent that a problem has no meaning except in a concrete setting. The very notion of taking some artificially contrived test is nonsensical."**
> Coch 2010

So much caution has to be exercised when administering and interpreting such assessment processes with different cultural groups that major validity questions are raised on every occasion.

So why do it?...

Testing conditions and interpretation of test results influence the IQ measure and other psychometric outcomes.
It has been shown that the outcome of any IQ test or psychometric procedure can depend on familiarity with the test materials, with the testing procedure and also with the examiner.

> **"No one would believe until I demonstrated it with controls that the IQ scores of pupils from an open air school could be lifted 10 points or so by thawing them out on the hot water pipes for half an hour before testing."**
> Head of Special School, cited in Galloway and Goodwin, 1979

Emotional tension and anxiety have also been indicated as factors affecting test scores. If being tested makes you highly anxious then performance is impaired and scores are lower.

One US experiment, asking 99 school psychologists to independently score an IQ test from identical records, resulted in IQs ranging from 63 (mild learning difficulties) to 117 (gifted) for the same individual. This indicates the critical role of the tester's attitudes, qualifications, and instructions on testing. In addition, differences in the interpretation of test scores for entire groups have been documented (Ropers and Menzel, 2007).

Taken together, these observations highlight severe shortcomings in the very process of testing IQ. So why try?

What is Actually Being Measured?

IQ tests are psychometric tests, which only capture a few aspects of many the different 'intelligences' or 'systems of abilities' that make us human. These tests give no attention to: creative and practical intelligence; social, emotional and moral intelligence; lateral and radiant thinking. IQ tests are static, in that they ask what the child has learned rather than being dynamic and asking what the child achieves when, for example, given guided feedback. In truth, we need to learn a lot more than we currently know or understand is happening when a child appears unable to do the task we have set them on our intelligence test. Consider this comment from Paula Kluth (2009) writing about psychometric assessment of students on the autistic spectrum:

> **"For many individuals on the spectrum, especially those without reliable communication, there is no test that can measure what they know and can do. Therefore most of the instruments used in evaluations measure autistic symptoms as much as, if not more than, abilities. On top of the inadequacy of the instruments used in these assessments, many aspects of the evaluation process itself make accurate assessment challenging, if not impossible...many children and adults with autism cannot participate in many assessments due to movement problems, sensory differences or related difficulties. It is not uncommon for a student with significant disabilities to get a low score on an instrument because she did not have a reliable pointing response, but was able to point. In other words, when asked to point to a monkey, some students point to a giraffe instead, even though they**

know which image is the monkey. This type of problem with motor planning is widely reported by people with autism"

The Misuse of IQ Assessment

A central criticism of intelligence tests is that psychologists and educators use these tests to distribute the limited resources of our society. Such test results are used to provide so called rewards such as special classes for gifted students, admission to college and employment, or, at the opposite end of opportunity - special education placement. Those who do not qualify for these resources, based on intelligence test scores, may feel angry as if the tests are denying them opportunities for success. Many negative predispositions have been initiated, aspirations lowered and self-fulfilling prophecies created.

Unfortunately, intelligence test scores have not only become associated with a person's ability to perform certain tasks, but also with self-worth. At worst such assessments have been used to wrongly place pupils from ethnic minority cultures in special schools and units. As far back as 1968 this was reported in ILEA and elsewhere where pupils from an African-Caribbean background were particularly over represented in special education.

The PLASC and School Level Annual School Census (2002) revealed that African-Caribbean pupils were over represented in Pupil Referral Units (5.8% compared with 1.5% in mainstream schools). Of even more relevance to the misuse of psychometrics was the finding that 3.6% of Pakistani pupils were in Special Schools. Could this have anything to do with other factors such as pupils living in poverty? Or are some pupils still being assessed and doing badly on culturally biased psychometric tests?

Dyson and Gallannaugh (2008) have considered the disproportional presence of students from different social groups in the UK special needs system. They argue that this disproportionality is the reality in England, as in the United States.

Single Score too Limited

Many intelligence tests produce a single intelligence score. This single score is inadequate to describing the multidimensional nature of human intelligence. Another problem with a single score is the fact that individuals with similar intelligence test scores can vary greatly in their expression of these talents. Two people can have identical scores on intelligence tests. Although both people

have the same test score, one person may have obtained the score because of strong verbal skills while the other may have obtained the score because of strong skills in perceiving and organising various tasks i.e. they are actually very different in how they prefer to perceive and process the world but the single score completely obscures this difference.

Testing Only a Sample of Behaviours

Intelligence tests only measure a sample of behaviours or situations in which assumed intelligent behaviour is revealed. Most intelligence tests do not measure a person's everyday functioning, social knowledge, mechanical skills, and/or creativity. The format of intelligence tests does not capture the complexity and immediacy of real life situations. Intelligence tests have been criticised for their limited ability to predict non-test or non-academic intellectual abilities.

Problems with the use of IQ Testing with Disabled Children and Adults.

Linda S. Siegel (1992), professor in the Department of Educational Psychology and Special Education at the University of British Columbia in Vancouver, Canada proposes that we abandon the IQ test in our work with disabled children.

According to most definitions, although they are not conclusive, intelligence is made up of the skills of logical reasoning, problem solving, critical thinking, and adaptation. This seems reasonable, until one examines the content of the actual IQ tests. Intelligence, as tested in all IQ tests, includes virtually none of the skills implicated in the above definition of intelligence.

To support her statement, Siegel gives a detailed analysis of the subtests of the *Wechsler Intelligence Scale for Children-Revised* (WISC-R). This IQ test is composed of Verbal and Performance sections, and is often used in diagnosis of learning difficulties. In each subtest of the Verbal Scale, scoring is in varying degrees, dependent on specific knowledge, vocabulary, expressive language and memory skills. In the Performance Scale, visual-spatial abilities, fine motor coordination, perceptual skills, and in some subtests speed, are essential for scoring. As Siegel rightly points out, IQ tests measure, for the most part, what a person has *learned*, not what he or she is capable of doing in the future.

There is an additional problem in the use of IQ tests with individuals with learning impairments. According to Siegel it is a paradox that IQ scores are required of disabled people because many of these persons have difficulty in one or more of the component skills that are part of these IQ tests, memory, language, fine motor skills, and so on. The effect is that they may end up having a lower IQ score than a person who does not have such problems, even though they may both have identical reasoning and problem-solving skills. A lower IQ score, therefore, may be a result of a particular learning impairment, a particular set of demands on your capacity to process information – the trouble is that the low IQ is then seen as a limit to all that you do.

Importance of Speed and Action for High Scoring on Tests

Most psychometric assessments are timed by using a stop watch. If you are slow because of movement differences or learning style you will do worse at the assessments. If doing things is hard for you because of any kind of physical impairment or difference then you will score less well against norms created using a 'typical' population.

Wait Time

Many of the questions or non-verbal activities used in psychometric tests allow only a limited time for a response from the person being tested. If this time is exceeded by the person no score is given for that item – the protocol says they get '0'. This aspect of testing is of course directly prejudicial to many disabled learners and in particular those with the kind of motor planning difficulties that are often associated with the label of autism. What we end up measuring here is the extent of a child's motor impairment – not their 'intelligence' – it is always entirely possible that they understood what was required by the test, but were unable to organise their response in the time allowed. These learners need us to *wait*. Waiting is one of the key tools in how we provide any support, but one of the hardest to do.

The Medical Model Dominates Thinking

IQ scores and psychometric test results are clinically focused on the child or young person's deficits especially if they have additional support needs. They provide one answer to the vexing question 'What is wrong with you?'

"I scored relatively high in an IQ test when I was a child. Since then I have done many, many, many, very, very, very stupid things in my life. I still wonder what that test has to do with intelligence or understanding at all."
Alex Wien, Austria, 2009

One of the most absurd and disrespectful uses of the IQ score is when it is used to describe a person's 'mental age'. Thus a disabled 16 year old can be described as having 'a mental age of 2' and this means that what they achieved on a test was in line with what a 2 year old typically functioning child achieves. Such summary descriptions are still widely used in the media and in professional reporting here in the UK and beyond. Just pause and think about this teenager with his so-called mental age of 2. He has – like all of us – lived a life, made choices and mistakes, enjoyed friends and endured hardships, collected memories. He is nothing like any two-year old any of us has ever met. Enough said?

The Concept of Least Dangerous Assumption

Many people are under the false assumption that intelligence tests measure a person's inborn or biological intelligence and that this is set in stone and can never change, that they have a fixed potential. In fact intelligence test scores are based on an individual's performance on that day with whoever administered the test and tell us nothing more than how it was for that person on that day when they were asked to do certain things under those conditions.

Disabled people are people first. Due to the presence of an impairment, a person may act, get around, look, dance, smile, read, learn, show what she knows, or communicate, *differently*. The key here is that this is a difference and not a deficiency. As humans, we are all alike only in that we are all different. The fact that society tends to create a hierarchy of these differences, by labelling some of them as deficiencies, is a manifestation of an out-dated paradigm plagued by prejudice. This inherent prejudice against disabled people means that some differences will be defined as deficiencies and looked down upon by all of those who perceive themselves to be higher up on the social ladder.

Anne Donnellan (1994), identified why this old paradigm is not sufficient and needs to be replaced by a more humanistic and respectful one. The key to the new paradigm is the concept of the "Least Dangerous Assumption."

Rossetti and Tashie (2006) have provided an excellent overview of this concept which we reproduce here in an edited form:

The Least Dangerous Assumption states that in the absence of absolute evidence, it is essential to make the assumption that, if proven to be false, would be least dangerous to the individual. Rossetti and Tashie explain that the "absence of evidence can never be absolute evidence of absence," and as such, it is always safest and most respectful to make the least dangerous assumption.

Consider it this way. If I were to go fishing for a week and not catch any fish, there would be two assumptions that could be made. First, I could say that there are no fish in the lake since I did not catch any, and I know what I am doing. Or, second, I could say simply that I did not catch any fish that week, and I will keep on trying. The first assumption seems rather arrogant, while the second one is more realistic and respectful. (There is a third assumption that I could make which would be that I am not a good fisherman, but we won't go there). The same holds true for students with severe additional needs. Imagine a child who does not talk with spoken words and moves around using a wheelchair. Her teachers have worked with her for a month and have not yet seen any evidence of what she understands. In fact, they wonder if she knows or is aware of anything at all. These teachers can make one of two assumptions. They can assume that "what you see is what you get" and that this child does not know anything, that her brain is as empty as that lake. As such, they can educate her in a way that reflects those assumptions, perhaps in segregated classes or regular classes with low or no expectations. Now imagine her as she graduates and uses a communication device to say: "Why did you treat me so poorly? I am smart and you wasted twelve years of my life"! A very dangerous assumption was made, with results that none of us would desire.

Now, consider the second (least dangerous) assumption. These same teachers can recognise that differences in her movement are differences and not deficiencies. They can assume that she knows a great deal and just is not currently able to show what she knows. Her brain is as full of knowledge and potential as that lake is of fish, but they just have not been able to reel anything in yet. As such,

her schooling would reflect these high expectations and she would be considered and respected as a valued member of her school and classes. Now again, imagine her twelve years later at graduation, using her communication device to say: "Thank you from the bottom of my heart to all of my teachers who believed in me and made me feel as if I truly belonged and treated me like all of my classmates." This is the least dangerous assumption, one that results in a young woman who can celebrate her full and fulfilling life.

But consider a third scenario as well. What if we never come up with a way for this young woman to communicate her intelligence? What if, after twelve years as a valued and respected student in all general education classes, we still do not know exactly what she has learned and knows? What harm was done? What was lost? Nothing. And that truly is the least dangerous assumption.

Understanding the concept of least dangerous assumption and acting on it are two different things. The idea of considering all people as capable and intelligent may not come naturally to some people due to the influence of society's prejudices against disabled people. Most well-intentioned adults and professionals have been taught to believe in the out-dated paradigm and, therefore, may make very dangerous assumptions about disabled students. Many people's first impressions of disabled people are tainted by years of societal prejudice and media portrayals of what is enviable and worthwhile. While the power of these experiences is strong, we can no longer allow this to serve as a justification for the perpetuation of the prejudices against disabled students or adults. Remind yourself that your prejudice is evident every time you assume that a person who does not use their voice - who cannot talk - has therefore little or no understanding.

The question we should all be asking ourselves is: "Do you really believe that the disabled individual is a valued, competent and unique person?" Think long and hard about that question. If you cannot honestly answer "Yes", then the next question is simply, "Why?" Think about your beliefs, your experiences, and the prejudice you have been taught. Ask yourself how you can change those dangerous assumptions and mindsets. Talk with people who are the friends, parents, siblings, lovers, and colleagues of disabled people. Listen to people who have been segregated or devalued because of the way they look or move or communicate. Learn everything you can about the many ways people communicate and get around and show us who they are and what they know.

Introduce yourself to people who had labels of 'severe learning difficulty' while in school, who now are able to communicate their thoughts and feelings and tell us all, loud and clear: "I am intelligent!" Recognise your prejudices and work through them. It will not be as difficult as it first seems. And you will never again make assumptions about people that result in the loss of opportunity, experience, or respect.

All people are people first. Everyone belongs to this wonderful life. No one should have to conform to someone else's standards before they are told that they are "good". We all belong. We all have strengths and weaknesses and our own individual potential to be great people and to live the lives we want. We can all lead happy and fulfilling lives, supported by those around us to be successful adults. It is up to all of us to examine our own core beliefs and to spread the word of the least dangerous assumption. We can no longer allow the justification of a prejudice that is so dangerous. Now is definitely the time to believe that all people are valued individuals with limitless potential. Keep on fishing - the lake is overflowing!!!!

So Does Intelligence Really Exist?

Intelligence does not exist as any kind of single entity or fixed potential. What else can we conclude about intelligence from the above?

- Intelligence cannot safely be reduced to a single measure

- Language and culture impact upon an individual's performance on any kind of psychometric test

- Movement differences and difficulties including issues with spoken language make such testing invalid and unreliable

- Intelligence measures are only dealing with experiences the tested person has had, they do not truly access underlying processes

- Intelligence assessment is based on highly questionable assumptions about thought and language.

The concept of 'multiple intelligences' (Gardner, 1983) is one useful way to consider thinking and problem solving processes as it at least points to the validity of a number of other ways of thinking (see below for more detail).

Or perhaps we should simply refer to specific thinking, linguistic, memory and problem solving processes without ever trying to bundle them up as one entity. We certainly should be wary of giving more value and credence to certain skills over others such as verbal over non-verbal, for instance.

Such a stance will call for more tentative, sophisticated ways of sketching out how someone operates in the world. Such sketching will need to be done in collaboration with those who know and love the person themselves and with their full participation. The tools used for such sketching may need to be more humble than the oppressive pseudo-scientific assessment tools of the past, but in turn are likely to be more useful and respectful. Could our sketches evolve into painted portraits?

Let us live with uncertainty, accept the messiness of the unknown and always assume that far more is present and possible when we hold back our limiting assumptions.

Practical Implications

The following points are worth consideration:

- Ask those who love a person or who spend most time with them to describe their strengths, gifts and needs. This is where true wisdom about a person exists. Structured questions may help and shared reflection and theory building after collecting stories may enrich a picture and better inform decisions and strategies.

- Beware of dangerous assumptions when assessing. Always assume competence when in doubt or when movements are difficult for a person.

- Work together with someone who has skills in augmentative or facilitative communication when trying to understand someone who does not use their voice.

- Paint or sketch portraits in words and images of the whole person and their context. Instead of trying to be the pseudo scientific objective tester we should adopt tools more familiar to the artist creating a portrait. (O'Brien 2002)

  Portrait painting will demand a range of different and more nuanced tools. We will be searching for what is healthy, capacity

and strength. This will involve us in genuinely listening to children or co-constructing a narrative with them.

This means reshaping the relationship between the psychologist, teacher or other would be assessor and the learner to arrive at an end product which influences future dialogues between the young person and those closest to him or her. To deepen the conversations we might have about that young person and their inclusion/place in the world. Details are given of the particular – the complexity and detail of another's experiences are documented in the hope that readers will see themselves in it even if it is exotic.

We only truly understand if we feel some sense of connection or identification with the person in the picture or story– stand in their shoes of the child with autism – nobody sees themselves in the generalisations of the 'Triad'. Context is a source of understanding – not a source of data distortion. Behaviour may give us a clue – but it is the meanings people attach to the behaviours that ought really to concern us.

The standard is authenticity rather than 'truth' so there is never a single story – many could be told. The narrowest stories about individuals are drawn from the psychometric encounter – "Kevin has a mental age of 2 years"

- Make use of criterion referenced or curriculum-based assessment to inform planning. How is a child progressing in relation to what they are being taught as opposed to presumed underlying intellectual processes? One of the aims of criterion referencing is to focus on individual, differentiated assessment. By moving away from norm-referencing, to a system which describes what students know, understand and can do, assessments can be used to provide feedback and to inform future teaching and learning needs.

- Use authentic assessment processes that respect context and learning. This is a form of assessment in which students are asked to perform real-world tasks that demonstrate meaningful application of essential knowledge and skills.

- Use the wider frame suggested by the work being done on 'Multiple Intelligences' and always notice and respect diverse Learning Styles.

The theory of multiple intelligences was developed in 1983 by Dr. Howard Gardner, professor of education at Harvard University. It suggests, in line with this chapter, that the traditional notion of intelligence, based on I.Q. testing, is far too limited. Instead, Dr. Gardner proposes eight different intelligences to account for the broader range of human potential in children and adults. These intelligences are:

- Linguistic intelligence ("word smart"):
- Logical-mathematical intelligence ("number/reasoning smart")
- Spatial intelligence ("picture smart")
- Bodily-kinaesthetic intelligence ("body smart")
- Musical intelligence ("music smart")
- Interpersonal intelligence ("people smart")
- Intrapersonal intelligence ("self smart")
- Naturalist intelligence ("nature smart")

- Engage in participant observation, which has a long and respected history in the world of anthropology. Participant observation is the direct involvement of the anthropologist in the activities of the people in that society, so that instead of just observing the people, the anthropologist is able to get a more hands on experience of how these people live their lives. The main advantages of participant observation are that it allows the anthropologist to obtain a deeper and more experienced insight on the activities that the individuals of a society perform and the ways in which they think and that it also allows anthropologists to gain a good overview of how and why a society functions. Meaning exists internal to situations if we can open ourselves to this meaning and express this. Who are the participants who will have best knowledge about a child or young person? How long will we need to be part of a young person's life to get a real handle on who they are and what they bring.

- Always respect the **social model of disability**. The social model of disability proposes that barriers and prejudice and exclusion

by society (purposely or inadvertently) are the ultimate factors defining who is disabled and who is not in a particular society.

Hard Questions

- How can we be sure what a person knows and thinks when they have no reliable means of communication?

- What needs to happen in order for a wider range of facilitated and augmented forms of communication to be readily accepted by educators and wider society as authentic?

- How can we lose the concept of 'intelligence' given it is so embedded in academic assessments and more widely in western culture? What can we replace this notion with?

Resources

- The definitive work on Movement Difference and the Least Dangerous Assumption is by Martha Leary and Anne Donnellan (1995) 'Movement Differences and Diversity in Autism' DRI Press, Wisconsin – contact Inclusive Solutions for ordering details.

- Also worth checking out is Steven Jay Gould's (1995) book 'The Mismeasure of Man' London, Norton and Co. Described as 'a masterwork, a ringing answer to those who would classify people, rank them according to their supposed genetic gifts and traits' The ultimate debunking of simplistic notions of intelligence.

The Fifth Key: Learning

> "Real learning is about being open and excited by ideas and the exchange of ideas. We can't learn if we don't feel good about who we are because it will be repetition and superficial. It won't get integrated into who we are. So I think we need to feel good and accepted for who we are, then we can take in what we need to know and integrate it into ourselves."
>
> Maresa McKeith (2009)

Who needs to learn differently for inclusion to be possible? The children? The adults? How does anyone learn? Can we get better at accommodating all learners? Could we better tune in to individual learning styles of children who are hard to include?

We must remember that at least 80% of all learning is by imitation. This starts with babies and carries on through life. Brain imaging is helping some understand how this works. (Arbib et. al., 2000).

As far back as the 1900s, Maria Montessori was one of many educationalists who argued for natural opportunities for children to learn from each other knowing the power of imitation. In her view adults should prepare the way but then step back and keep out of the way, as servants to masters. We could learn much from this perspective today in the traditional 'special needs' world that has grown up with all its dependencies, low assumptions and restrictions.

This is why educating children in mainstream schools makes so much such educational sense quite apart from the human rights dimension. Children learn from each other by copying. Let us give them a great range of role models to help them develop communication, learning and social skills.

In the previous chapter we outlined why we must not be confused by notions of intelligence and fixed potential. Such ideas limit our imaginations and sense of what is really possible.

> "Scientific observation has established that education is not what the teacher gives; education is a natural process spontaneously carried out by the human individual, an is acquired not by listening to words but by experiences upon the environment. The task of the teacher becomes that of preparing a series of motives of cultural activity, spread over a specially prepared environment, and then refraining from obtrusive interference. Human teachers can only help the great work that is being done, as servants help the master. Doing so, they will be witnesses to the unfolding of the human soul and to the rising of a New Man who will not be a victim of events, but will have the clarity of vision to direct and shape the future of human society."

Montessori, 1905

How Does Anyone Learn?

This question has perplexed psychologists and educators for many years. The full answer to this question is beyond the scope of this book but we can at least lift the lid and see the areas that are key to inclusion. Anyway, what does anyone committed to inclusion need to know about learning?

How does anyone learn?

People – places – activities – interests

Context – meaning – situational

Sensory – hands and body – listening – movement – communication – smell – taste – tactile

Emotional experience

Associations and connections

Knowing individual needs

Relationships

One off learning- generalising to different situations- adaptation

Cognitive Perspective

Understanding or comprehension does not necessarily lead to learning, at least, not to learning of a meaningful, useful kind. How many people can remember the actual words of books they read five years ago?

People do not ordinarily remember much of the exact information they read. Instead, they learn the "gist" of it. They select. They use selected portions of the information to address issues important to them.

The vast bulk of information we are exposed to, or read is simply forgotten. We discard the details. Once new information has been comprehended by linking it to what is already known, new information can then be learned through activities, which enrich the connections between new, and older knowledge.

Anyone can convert "comprehended information" into "learned information," through such activities as play, dialogue, taking notes, summarising, outlining, making analogies, relating the information to yourself personally, creating mental imagery, and similar activities known as elaboration. Grow (1996) describes the learning process as:

- **Elaboration** - any method of "thinking about new ideas and prior knowledge together" so the two become more deeply connected. (Derry, 1990)
- **Learning** takes place when the new information becomes a part of the existing knowledge network.
- When elaborated and richly integrated, the new knowledge becomes **meaningful and useful**.
- The new knowledge can **fit into** the existing knowledge network or it can **modify** that network

Knowledge can be called "meaningful" only after it is richly interconnected with related knowledge. Knowledge can be called "useful" only if you can access it under real life situations.

Meaningful knowledge is filed and cross-referenced with other knowledge to which it is connected. Useful knowledge is filed and cross-referenced so that you can find it when you need it.

Andy learns to use the word 'moon' in the classroom in response to a picture and he links this with looking up at the moon and stars but without the words for what they are. When he hears his mum use the word the next evening whilst looking at the night sky he makes the connection and uses the word himself again.

Apart from this cognitive model of learning, other models of how children and adults learn have been influenced by research in a number of areas of academic and research psychology but the main positions are as follows.

Behavioural Psychology

Knowledge and skills can be broken down into component parts and it is the teacher's job to do this for the learner. The teacher then teaches each element and gives the student sufficient repetition until the learner can give a 'positive response'. The student will generally receive the same instruction as everyone in the class, but if assessment shows that the student requires further help, then an additional programme with smaller steps over a longer time scale will be provided. Rewards and consequences as responses to learning, inspired by studies of animals are at the heart of this perspective. This approach can be criticised for being too simplistic and reductionist as a good model for the complexity of human learning. However this approach continues to be very influential. The work of BF Skinner has dominated this field.

BF Skinner 1904 - 1990

Skinner said that there are five main obstacles in learning:

• People have a fear of failure.
• The task is not broken down into small enough steps.
• There is a lack of directions.
• There is also a lack of clarity in the directions.
• Positive reinforcement is lacking.

Skinner suggests that any age-appropriate skill can be taught using five principles to remedy the above problems

- Give the learner immediate feedback.
- Break down the task into small steps.
- Repeat the directions as many times as possible.
- Work from the most simple to the most complex tasks.
- Give positive reinforcement.

Developmental Psychology

A learner constructs meanings by getting to grips with the particular problems in hand. Private problem solving is very important and a teacher should provide the necessary stimulus material and opportunities for the individual student to learn something new. A student will not progress without plenty of practice in the activities that have already been mastered. In particular a child will only be able to 'get' an idea when she has reached a certain stage of maturity and the teacher's job is to be aware of that and to decide when the learner is 'ready' to move on. This has been problematic when children do not develop along a smooth developmental path but educators are waiting for a stage to emerge, for example speaking before introducing skills of a perceived higher stage such as spelling.

This perspective has been strongly influenced by the work of Piaget and Vygotsky.

J Piaget 1896 – 1980

Piaget (1937) proposed four stages that all children would go through. Piagetian's accounts of development have been challenged on several grounds. First, as Piaget himself noted, development does not always progress in the smooth manner his theory seems to predict. 'Decalage', or unpredicted gaps in the developmental progression, suggest that the stage model is at best a useful approximation. More broadly, Piaget's theory is 'domain general', predicting that cognitive maturation occurs concurrently across different domains of knowledge (such as mathematics, logic, understanding of physics, of language, etc).

Lev Vygotsky, 1869 -1934

Vygotsky's notion of 'zone of proximal development' (ZPD) as where and what we are about to learn has stimulated much thinking. ZPD is Vygotsky's term for the range of tasks that are too difficult for the child to master alone but that can be learned with guidance and assistance of adults or more-skilled children. The lower limit of ZPD is the level of skill reached by the child working independently. The upper limit is the level of additional responsibility the child can accept with the assistance of an able instructor.

The ZPD captures the child's cognitive skills that are in the process of maturing and can be accomplished only with the assistance of a more-skilled person. Scaffolding is a concept closely related to the idea of ZPD. Scaffolding is changing the level of support. Over the course of a teaching session, a more-skilled person adjusts the amount of guidance to fit the child's current performance. Dialogue is an important tool of this process in the zone of proximal development. In a dialogue, the unsystematic, disorganised, and spontaneous concepts of a child are met with the more systematic, logical and rational concepts of the skilled helper.

This perspective emerged from the work of Piaget and Vygotsky (above). From this position all learners are viewed as educable and are helped in their learning through discussion and other social interaction, including interaction with a more experienced learner or teacher. There is no fundamental difference between the learning of children and that of adults. Rather than waiting for a student to be ready to learn, a teacher is finding out what the learner thinks in order to guide and support what the learner is trying to do next. By talking with the teacher and their peers and obtaining other support, a learner is able to grasp ideas and new understandings that they could never arrive at on their own.

Social Constructivist Psychology

We find the latter two models to be most useful to those working on inclusion. In our experience most learning is developmental and importantly takes place in the social context of relationships. These say that we should consider disability and developments as the product of larger systems of relationships, not as things that happen *'in the head'*.

"The development or disablement of a child can no longer be considered a "given" at birth or at diagnosis. Instead, we can recognize that these are processes played out in a larger context over which we all have influence. When children experience movement differences due to perceptual/regulatory problems in their nervous systems, these differences make it difficult for them to connect successfully with the people and objects that make up their environment, and their world may become very narrow. The nature, quality, and developmental appropriateness of the interactions which we help them to experience becomes of vital importance, since these interactions will establish a system of feedback for their emotional and cognitive development, which in turn will enhance their ability to make future connections."
Donnellan, Anne. M., and Martha R. Leary, 1990

Key relationships for pupils with additional needs will be with:

- The teachers, who lead, design and deliver the curriculum to which pupils are exposed.
- The other pupils with whom they are educated.
- The involvement of parents and carers in the education process.
- The additional supporting adults who may be present as personal assistants or teaching assistants.

These relationships can be rich and productive or can negatively impact on learning for the following reasons:

- Instruction which is boring or under stimulating
- Additional adults providing too much suffocating support and creating dependency
- Where peers are blocked from being involved in individual support and modeling in areas such as communication and learning.

We have learned that learning is strongest and richest for high need pupils where:

- Learning is meaningful and engaging – linked to personal interests where possible
- Other pupils are actively involved in cooperative and collaborative learning
- There is recognition that learning is located in specific situations and needs work for generalisation to other places to occur
- Other pupils are involved in creative learning support strategies
- Close teamwork between key adults including parents and carers and individual teachers is creative and allows for flexible problem-solving
- Where individual learning programs are in position, targets are meaningful; strategies are rich and where learning takes place is clear.
- Such programmes are reviewed regularly and maintain vitality and shared ownership between all involved.

A very useful framework of learning supports for a challenging situation around issues of behaviour, habit or movement difference has been proposed by Donnellan and Leary (2006) and includes the following:

You are okay.
Let us work on this together.
Let us create a plan to support you.

How respectful are these statements? So much better than a group of professionals moving into an adjacent room to work out what's wrong with you and how they are going to fix you! What would you prefer?

In more detail Leary and Donnellan describe the framework as:

- *You're OK- Each person is OK just the way they are. Like all of us, people may want to change things in their lives, learn new skills, fit in, etc. Support includes recognition of a person's current attempts to participate.*
- *Let's Collaborate- Effective support includes the person in choice of goals for change and preferences for learning.*

- ***Support to Organize*** - *focuses on consideration of how our assumptions and people's symptoms affect the way in which you support a person to learn new skills, e.g. - using the right prompts - respectful application of a discrete trial format in natural contexts. Overview of some of the "accommodations" that people have used successfully to get around persistent difficulties.*

(Donnellan and Learey, 2006 Conference input)

Activity

Imagine reversing your car into a small car parking space at the first attempt. List factors that would help and hinder you.

The answers to this question invariably give an excellent overview of what a framework for supported learning in any place of learning should look like. Answers are likely to include the following....

Not pressured
No one criticising from the passenger seat
No one trying to help me too much
Quiet with no radio or voices
Time to work it out myself
Practice
Familiarity with the vehicle

Everyone has a dominant sense that they prefer to use to learn: or do they?

Pupils often attribute their learning difficulties to the form in which course material is presented at school. Some pupils find they have difficulties learning in situations where the course material is only presented orally, while others report similar difficulties when the material is primarily in written form. Still others hate group discussion, experience difficulty with ideas presented in graphics or without any associated concrete experiences.

Learners of any age do seem to take in and process information in different ways: by seeing and hearing, reflecting and acting, reasoning logically and intuitively, analysing and visualising, steadily or in fits and starts. Teaching methods also vary. Some instructors lecture, others demonstrate or lead students to self-discovery; some focus on principles and others on applications; some emphasise memory and others understanding. There are clearly interactions and styles that may be situation specific. Needless to say educators choosing to stay in one mode of operation does not seem to be helpful for pupils with additional needs. Teachers, who insist on talking at length, or having long periods of copying from wallboards and so on, may invite problems into their learning environment.

In a Scottish secondary school, Stewart, a tactile 14 year old, could only sit still in his maths lessons when his teacher discovered a particular piece of fur that he loved to stroke. She simply stuck the fur underneath his desk and he was allowed to stroke this whenever he needed to. This prevented him rocking forward and backwards on his chair distracting other students.

When mismatches exist between the learning styles of most students in a class and the teaching style of a teacher or trainer, the learners may become bored and inattentive. They may get discouraged about the curriculum and themselves. Learners may act out, or refuse to be present. Teachers, confronted by low attainments, unresponsive or hostile groups and poor attendance often know something is not working. They may become overly critical of their students (making things even worse) or begin to wonder if they are in the right profession. Most seriously, society loses potentially excellent professionals.

Jarvis and was an eight-year-old boy who always wanted to be on the go. He was a clearly kinaesthetic learner who loved physical activities but could not bear to be sitting for long periods at a desk. His creative teacher provided him with a small exercise-peddling bike that could sit under his desk and he could peddle whenever he wished to. This worked well for everyone.

To overcome these problems, educators should strive for a balance of teaching and learning methods (as opposed to trying to teach

each student exclusively according to his or her preferences.) If the balance is achieved, all learners will be taught partly in a manner they prefer, which leads to an increased comfort level and willingness to learn, and partly in a less preferred manner, which provides practice and feedback in ways of thinking and solving problems which they may not initially be comfortable with but which they will have to use to be flexible citizens of the world.

> In a UK primary school, a gifted infant teacher was troubled by too many children approaching her through literacy time. She introduced a system whereby she wore a coloured hat, bright red when she did not want to be approached. The scheme worked extremely well for all students including one with autism who needed very clear messages. This visual approach soon became popular across the school with many staff becoming very creative using a range of headdresses from policemen's helmets to exotic African headgear!

Finally - beware of teaching predominantly through your own learning style, for example speaking/auditory. This is a very easy trap for any educator to drop into…

Gregorc Model of Learning Styles

We think that Dr Anthony Gregorc (1998) has created a useful model for understanding learning style, proposing differences in the way people perceive and order data.

He suggests a perception continuum from Concrete to Abstract

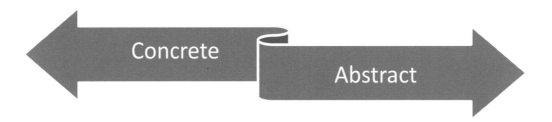

In our training with educators we ask people to stand along an imaginary line and explore the differences that exist at the extremes.

He also suggests a line or continuum between on the theme of ordering.

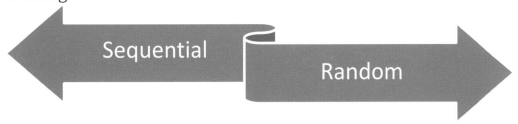

We also ask people to stand on these lines and reflect on how they go shopping, or how they tidy their home. Differences can be hilarious or mortifying for individuals as they reflect on this.

The lines cross creating for Gregorc four distinctive learning styles:

Concrete Sequential Learner

These learners prefer direct, hands-on activities, tactile methods, step-by-step instructions, and real life examples. This learner is likely to respond well to an imposed 'one size fits all' curriculum.

Instructional methods: workbooks with detailed instructions, diagrams, flowcharts, computer-assisted instruction, documentation, and hands-on activities.

Concrete Random Learner

These learners prefer a trial-and-error approach, with breakthroughs due to intuitive insight. They like a stimulus-rich environment. They thrive on competition, especially if they can use their wits. These learners rarely accept anything on outside authority. They are initiators of change and tend to be impulsive. They do not like to read directions and dislike structure. Many boys with emotional and behavioural needs have this style and are not served well by a curriculum that favours the concrete sequential approach.

Instructional methods: independent study, computer games and simulations, multimedia, and "playing" with software.

Abstract Sequential Learner

These learners prefer a highly verbal, logical and analytical approach based on intellect. Their motto is "knowledge is power." They like solitude, prefer well-organized material, and are highly

skeptical. They have trouble picking up subtle nonverbal cues and dislike distractions. They will accept change only after much deliberation. They like written, verbal, and visual instruction.

Instructional methods: lectures, reading, outlines, conducting Internet searches, email, and audiotapes. Abstract sequential learners may enjoy searching the Internet for information as well as asynchronous communication because they have time to think about their responses.

Abstract Random Learner

These learners like to focus on relationships and their emotions. They respond to visual methods of instruction, group discussion, and time for reflection. They may be uncomfortable with distance education because it does not include the emotional involvement of meeting face to face, unless the instructor is careful to build rapport as part of the learning experience. They enjoy evaluating personal experiences.

Instructional methods: video clips, group discussion, videoconferencing, television, case studies, chatrooms, and guest speakers.

Individuals with such different styles can often find it hard to relate to others with contrasting styles. Clashes, battles and other conflict can easily occur when styles clash.

> *Why do you need to go down every aisle when supermarket shopping?*

> *Why are you always so vague, what exactly are we meant to be doing?*

Improving our understanding of such individual differences can only help our educational processes and how well we include a wider, more diverse range of pupils.

Learners with challenging emotional and behavioural needs are often found to be those with random and concrete learning preferences. This finding has obvious practical implications for planning activities at all stages of a child or young person's education.

Exploring these individual preferences can be very rich and

generate much reflection on individual differences in learning but also in the way people engage with the world. We often ask people at extremes of the continuum to have a live discussion about how they would go about simple activities such as tidying, shopping or preparing for an exam. There are no right or wrong answers simply diverse ways of approaching similar activities. However the education system will favour certain styles in particular curriculum areas depending upon how they are delivered.

Surprisingly the Learning and Skills Research Centre (2004) could not find *any* published evidence addressing the benefits of self-knowledge of learning styles or the alignment of Gregorc-type learning and teaching styles.

Still the concepts are certainly thought provoking and we have found them very useful in encouraging a deeper understanding of individual differences when approaching familiar tasks and activities.

We would argue that a discussion of learning styles may prove to be an excellent catalyst for individual, classroom, organisational or even wider systemic change in any place of learning.

What is Diversity?

We have all read enough mission statements that claim a key purpose of the organisation is to 'celebrate diversity'. What on earth does this mean? Once a month we will eat foods from another culture? We will buy some posters of women scientists? We will mark others' religious festivals in some way? Or could it come to mean that we become better at putting ourselves in the shoes of those who see the world in different ways from us? And, once we have understood it a little, give it equal recognition?

Consider this first person account from Maresa Mackeith, a young disabled person who does not speak with a conventional spoken voice, of the cognitive diversity within human experience:

> **"I want to talk about us, who can't talk, taking part in ordinary life. It's about learning real learning. It's about learning who we are, and how we think, and how we can contribute to the wider understanding of humanity. As a person who needs assistance to communicate."**
> MacKeith, 2009

Making Accommodations and Reasonable Adjustments

In the UK under the Special Educational Needs and Disability Act 2001 (SENDA), educational settings such as schools and colleges defined under the Act as 'responsible bodies' are required to make 'reasonable adjustments'.

This is to ensure that disabled students are not discriminated against or placed at a substantial disadvantage in all areas of educational life especially in relation to teaching and teaching resources.

- Arran needs to hold a small figure of Batman before he can settle calmly on the carpet to listen to the story.

- Kelly needs to pace backwards and forwards at the back of the room at least three times during a science lessons.

- Jamil uses a magnifier when working with written materials.

This means that it is now unlawful for institutions to treat a disabled person 'less favourably' than they treat or would treat a non-disabled person for a reason which relates to the persons' disability.

For example, it would be unlawful for an institution to turn a disabled person away, or refuse to provide accessible teaching materials if that person had dyslexia or were deaf. When learners are being formally assessed a range of accommodations can now be present. Take this Open College Network (2009) set of guidance about what might be needed in an exam on Religious Studies:

- Low vision aids, overlays
- Brailing of non-secure assessment material
- Amplification, taped questions and responses
- Supervised rest breaks
- Use of a Reader
- Use of an Amanuensis
- Use of a Practical Assistant
- Use of a Communicator
- Bilingual dictionaries with an allowance of additional time
- Transcription of a student's written responses
- Word processor
- Use of a Prompter

A reasonable adjustment might be any action that helps alleviate a substantial disadvantage. Making a reasonable adjustment might involve changing procedures, adapting curriculum, providing additional services (e.g. materials in large print), or altering the

physical environment. For example a pupil with autism might need a change in lighting in a room or a reduction in noise levels at certain times of the day. Such environmental accommodations would be seen as reasonable adjustments.

Many learners particularly those with autism will have sensory sensitivities. These will almost certainly require accommodations including:

- Changes to the environment, e.g. lights dimmed
- Individual adjustments or supports, e.g. a child wears headphones
- Opportunities to leave environment, e.g. a person leaves training room at lunchtime when smell becomes too strong for him to bear

Reasonable adjustments and accommodations to the learning situation make sense for everyone. Other learners often benefit from individual adjustments for classmates with respect to areas such as lighting, sound, delivery of instruction and so on.

> **"Emotional and cognitive development is a tightly-integrated, individual process which every child and adult must "own" -- that is, it can be facilitated but not forced. Interactions with the environment must make sense to the developing child, rather than being taught as a collection of isolated skills or rote performances. This process takes time: we can appreciate that there are no quick fixes and that undue attention to surface appearances (looking "normal") may have little developmental significance for the person with movement differences. The presence of a symptom is not just cause for deciding to eliminate it. Instead, decisions about intervention should be based on factors such as individual choice and safety. It is far more productive in the long run to adapt the environment and adjust our interactions to accommodate the person with movement differences."**
> Donnellan, Anne. M., and Martha R. Leary., 1990

Differentiation

In a differentiated classroom, students can expect to experience a wide range of strategies, learning experiences, and approaches. These strategies, formats, experiences, and approaches include, but are not limited to, cooperative learning, partner work, peer tutoring, drama, simulations, group problem solving, self-directed learning, project-based instruction, and games.

Kluth 2009 describes differentiation thus:

- *When a teacher allows students different ways to express their understanding of a novel (taking a written test, designing a piece of art related to the book, giving a speech comparing the novel to other works), she is differentiating instruction.*

- *When a teacher uses cooperative learning approaches and assigns students' roles that will challenge them as individuals, he is differentiating instruction.*

- *When a teacher provides students with a range of materials to teach immigration (travel documents, costumes, maps, interactive software), she differentiating instruction.*

- *When a teacher makes informed decisions when grouping students for instruction, he is differentiating instruction.*

For learning to occur with any sense of fulfillment and progress for a young person with additional learning needs, differentiation within the curriculum from the early years through to college years will be essential. The following is a useful way of thinking about levels of differentiation:

Differentiation will occur for all learners at 3 levels:

Standard: The norm; three levels of differentiation in all class groups. All, most, or some of what is taught will be learned so three levels of work set.

Extra: An extra level of differentiation is carried out for an individual pupil in a particular curriculum area

Alternative: Alternative differentiation. On very rare occasions curriculum areas will overlap (e.g. a pupil is given additional literacy work in a numeracy session)

Learning Priorities

What should a young person with additional needs learn? What is most important for them?

As increasing numbers of children and young people with significant and lifelong support needs are included in mainstream settings, there is a growing need for review procedures that incorporate longer term planning goals within their design.

By directing their parents and support team's attention to long term valued life outcomes (Giangreco, 1998) for students from the start, review and planning processes can go far beyond the outcomes of a typical IEP review meeting or the statutory annual review of a statement of special educational need.

This may not be for all students who have an Individual Education Plan (IEP); it is for use with the small number of students who have many areas of additional need, those for whom it can be difficult to prioritise and arrive at a manageable but relevant plan with clear targets. This approach may be a valuable addition to the Special Educational Needs Coordinator's toolkit and lead to more effective curriculum differentiation in the classroom.

Such a process begins by asking the parents and team to think about what we consider to be 'The eight big life priorities' (Note the similarity with 'Every Child Matters' Outcomes) for the young person in question:

- *Being safe and healthy*

- *Having a home now and in the future*

- *Enjoying meaningful relationships*

- *Being involved in decision-making and making choices*

- *Participating in meaningful activities: community/school/home*

- *Having a meaningful way of communicating*

- *Engaging in accessible learning opportunities*

- *Emotional and social development.*

Time spent exploring how 'the long view' might take shape under these eight headings is part of the processes that build and clarify

shared vision for the young person between the parents/carers and the educational team. Planning for more immediate educational goals is not undertaken until time has been spent considering the eight big questions and the direction they set. This process builds parental partnership and participation in the planning process and avoids the kind of criticisms (Dixon 1991) made of our traditional planning approaches with their emphasis on short term outcomes, present levels of functioning and what the young person is not able to do.

Drawing on the work of Michael Giangreco (1998) and elements of Essential Lifestyle Planning (Smull and Sanderson 2001) PLAN is a still unpublished work, the result of two years of development work and trialling by a group of 6 primary and secondary special educational needs co-ordinators working within mainstream schools in Nottingham city and supported by Inclusive Solutions.

PLAN: Individual Pupil Profile

From the priority areas you have selected and having completed the detailed analysis above the next step is to agree precise priorities and list these as areas for development. (The suggested maximum is 8 areas for development.)

For example the team might agree that a student has the following priorities in the area of 'Engaging in accessible learning opportunities'

- Uses Clock

- Uses Calendar

Then using the ratings:

- Stop (no evidence of development)

- Amber (emerging skills)

- Go (fully established)

Emerging skills or essential skills, where there is no evidence of development, should be prioritised and listed on the Pupil Profile under the headings Difficulties and Areas for Development

Strengths can readily be lifted from the detailed analysis and the 'About Me' profile. Additional items can be added that are considered essential within the student's particular school and community context. (See example on page 68)

INDIVIDUAL PUPIL PROFILE		
Name: DOB: Date of profile: Profiled by:		
Strengths	Difficulties	Areas for development

Throw away those tired old plans!...

Stop repeating the same target year after year for the same pupil. How many years will targets like 'must learn to sit still' or learn to listen for 5 minutes' or 'write the initial sound – b ' be repeated? It becomes mindless and not meaningful for all. Stop it now.

Record Keeping and Plans

Essential Lifestyle Planning

This is one approach which is more encouraging. It is more person centred, with more creative and respectful record keeping. This can be used with adults and children. Michael Smull (2000) describes the process for adults as follows:

- *Start with how the person wants to live*

- *Learn what is important to the person in everyday life*

- *Assess issues of health and safety*

- *Assess what the person might want to learn to get more of what is important*

- *Plan **with** the person*

- *Describe what is important to the person*

- *Describe what others need to know or do to support the person*

- *Addressing any issues of health or safety in the context of how the person wants to live*

- *Offer opportunities for learning that help the person get more of what the person wants*

- *As the person gets more of what is important in everyday life*

- *Look for opportunities for the person to spend time in places and doing things where they are welcomed by the others there*

- *As the person spends time where they are welcomed, look for opportunities to help establish and nurture relationships*

- *Seek to discover what the person might like in the future and help them move in that direction (Smull 2000)*

All About Me - www.inclusive-solutions.com/stephensbook.asp

This is an excellent booklet that has been written by a young person from Scotland with help from those who know him best and is a very accessible form of essential life style planning with children. The booklet features photos and great headings like:

- What I do for others
- What I am good at
- If I become distressed it would really help me if you could....
  And -

It would really help me if you could.......

Remind me to go to the toilet at regular intervals through the day.

Supervise me when I am in the toilet area.

If I am very involved in what I am doing I will leave it until the last possible minute.

Remind me to wash and dry my hands after I go to the toilet.

Although I know to do this I don't really see why it is so important.

I am full of mischief and love playing with water. I especially like watching water cascading out of an overflowing sink and will indulge this pleasure when given the opportunity to do so.

Remind me of the purpose of sitting in the dining room at lunchtime.

Supervise me closely when I am getting changed for PE.

I am able to change myself but have problems coordinating small buttons and hooks. I am however quite lazy and would much rather have someone else to wait on me hand and foot.

It would really help me if you could.......

Make sure I only eat and drink what my Mum and Dad supply (or what is on my green food list).

Foods containing Gluten or Casein turn me into a whirling dervish.

Help me identify the dangers within my environment. Sometimes my inquisitive nature gets the better of me and I will disregard even obvious dangers in my quest for knowledge.

If I see an interesting car on the other side of the road, I will go to investigate without checking to see if it is safe to cross.

Let me know what my plan for the day is and give me advance notice that things are about to change.

My main way of learning is watching others and then copying their role modelling. Once I have sussed out the situation and am sure I know what is expected of me I will become an eager participant.

Make sure my PECS book is always available to me and remind me to take it with me.

If I cannot explain what is wrong I become very frightened and frustrated. I feel like I have no control.

Reid, 2002

This work shows how important gifts and capacity are when planning for pupil's education. How useful if you meet Stephen for the first time ever? Person centred booklets like these are appearing all around the UK. They are getting names like *Personal Portfolio* or *Passport*. Develop your own for a child you know today!!

Babu's Plan is another example of person-centred thinking being used to profile a school age student. Created by Babu himself, his parents and friends, it was intended as a one page introduction to Babu for the many new adults he would meet as he transferred to secondary school at age 11.

Me

My name is Ayusman but everyone calls me Babu. I am from India and I moved to England when I was 5. I live in Wimbledon with my mum, dad and 3 year old brother, Jackie. I want to be an astronaut when I am older.

Words that describe me best

very friendly
always cheerful
helpful
kind

My strengths and talents

Numbers and calculations in my head.
My friends in primary school called me Mr Calculator.

I'm also really good at remembering dates and times.

I can remeber new facts well.

My favourite things

My favourite foods are chocolate, rice and vegetables.
I love travelling and visiting new countries.
I love the Guiness book of records and learning new facts.
My favourite subject is Maths.
I like watching shows about Space and nature.
I love going to Theme Parks like Thorpe Park.

An Ideal Day

My escort is on time to take me to school.
The other children don't argue or fight.
The class is quiet for me to listen to my teacher and do my work.
My teacher likes my work.
I play games like chase or be a goalie at lunchtime.
We use maps in Geography.
I have a Numeracy, ICT and Art class
I earn some House points
There is fish and rice for lunch

My fears and worries / Things I dont like

Sudden noises
When things suddenly change
When I don't know what's going to happen next.
When people are late
When people use too much language
I dont eat meat but I eat fish

Babu Basu

My Worst Possible Day

Traffic making me late for school.
Children being really noisy and misbehaving.
Lots of complex instructions that I don't understand.
No-one to help me get things organised.
Sitting too far from the board so I can't see it.
Noone to play with at lunchtime or not understanding the game.
Getting a detention.

Ways ABA support helps me

Leaving me to do the things I can but helping me when I am stuck.
Helping me in the playground as I find making new friends or understanding new games really hard.
ABA helps explain things in a way that I can understand and learn better.

What you can do to help me

I feel like everyone else but I sometimes need a little more help. If you could give me clear and simple instructions and repeat instructions to me that would be really good. Also, I find visual aids very helpful and if you could give me an idea of what we will be learning in the lesson before it starts that will help me get ready for it. Thank you

Labels and Diagnoses: Good or Bad?

Of all the conversations we have about inclusion and young disabled people, the confusion surrounding our use of labels seems endless. Is knowing and using child's label helpful to us or them? Or, as educators, should we avoid labels entirely leaving their use to those whose job it is to make diagnoses and predict what they think impairment will mean in the future?

How are we to talk about children and young people in a way that respects their individuality *and* their needs?

As ever, the answer to all these questions is: "It depends"
It depends on who is doing the asking and to what use the label is put. If we take the trouble to read what labelled young people them say about their label we will be in little doubt about what we should do. Here is Luke Jackson writing about how he first found out, at age 12, about his Asperger Syndrome.

> **"I first found out about Asperger Syndrome...from an article in The Guardian...The article had a checklist of certain behaviours that were considered to be traits of Asperger Syndrome. I was twelve years old when I first read this article. Mum had just plonked it in front of me as if she had done it by accident. As I read through the article my first reaction was relief. It was as if I had a weight lifted off my shoulders. I had every single 'symptom' on this checklist. I had finally found the reason why other people classed me as weird. It was not because I was clumsy or stupid. My heart lightened instantly and the constant nagging that had accompanied me all my life stopped immediately. I finally knew why I felt different, why I felt as if I was a freak, why I didn't seem to fit in. Even better it was not my fault!"**
> Jackson, 2002

This is an insider perspective on the issue of labels. And it is telling us that young people need the information that comes with their label to help them understand their difference, know it is not of their making and, crucially, reassure them there are many others in the world like them.

So far so good. And if it was just about the power of a label to help the person with the impairment and others understand difference then there would be very little to get concerned about. If only labels were just used in this way! It is not the label that's the problem it is how we use it. And when we use it in ways that diminish or seem to

suggest that all there is to know about a child or young person is implicit in their label; this is when we get into trouble.

Consider the following account given to us by a mother as she visits possible future mainstream schools for her 4-year-old daughter with autism. The visit seems to go well for the most part, the Head seems to be listening as the mother describes her daughters personality, her likes and dislikes and some of her particular needs. The meeting comes to a close and the head teacher signs off with this attempt at reassurance:

"I'm sure we'll be fine – We had an autistic a couple of years ago"

In that moment the mother's mind is made up for her. There is no way now she will be considering this school for her daughter. What went so wrong here? We can assume the head teacher was trying to communicate her good intentions.

So, in the midst all this confusion, what can we do to minimise our chances of giving offense? There is one very simple answer that should serve you well in most situations: *ask the person how they like to be known.* And be prepared to accept their Christian name as the answer...This is always better than assuming or trying to be politically correct about what words or descriptors you think you should use. On occasions you will find your assumed political correctness is either out of date or not accepted by the group you are trying to address.

We recently did some visioning work with a group of mothers and daughters whose identity we were careful to refer to as "travellers". Their head-shaking and facial expressions immediately told us we were off track. When we asked them how they liked to be known as a group their answer was immediate and straightforward: gypsies or Romany gypsies. Never mind the fact that we would likely have avoided using the word gypsy at all costs, assuming it to be insulting, when a marginalised minority reclaims a word and thus affirms their identity they are saying that a word much used to insult can now no more be a cause of shame; we can only follow their lead.

"Our professional roles will be restored to helping people to be who they want to be rather than in assessing who we think they are and getting them to accept our assessment as their reality"
Lovett, 1996

We spend much time working with groups, mainly of adults encouraging them to think more deeply about inclusive education and its importance. Learning is dear to our hearts-and it is hearts as often as minds that we often feel the need to appeal to. Inevitably this leads us to try and create empathy with students and their families.

Our Experience

In our experience of teaching adults and children the following varied learning and teaching processes are to be commended for impacting on a range of learning preferences:

- Surprise and anticipation
- Enthusiasm
- Short inputs-never longer than 3-4 minutes
- Movement around room
- Different group sizes and shapes
- Visual aides
- Graphic processes accompanying learning
- Supporting Music
- Dialogue between learners
- Challenge from teachers
- Short high quality Video pieces (no more than 12 minutes long)
- Drama and participation processes
- Use of photos and images as dominant communication in presentations
- Key words only in presentations

Practical Implications

- Do not bore anyone if you are in a teaching or training role whatever their age

- Respectful relationships nurture learning

- Use a positive framework of support that's starts with 'you are OK' for those with greatest learning needs

- Notice individual preferences and style

- Never, never, never make assumptions about how much or how little someone can learn

Hard Questions

- What do we do when it is very hard to understand what a learner's learning style is?

- How can we tell what the person is really learning?

- What is the most important learning experience for anyone going through the education system?

Resources

- Teachers Toolkit: Raise Classroom Achievement with Strategies for Every Learner (Ginnis, 2002. Crown House Publishing)

- http://differentiationdaily.com/
  Web resources for differentiation updated daily by Paula Kluth

The Sixth Key: The Intentional Building of Relationships

"The heart of successful inclusion is relationships."
Sapon Shevin, 2007

We used to think we could drop any pupil into a mainstream school, setting or community and friendships would form and everything would be just great. We now know this is not true. For inclusion to be a reality we will often have to work *intentionally* to create the conditions in which relationships are more likely to take root and grow. The more complex or challenging the young person is, the more planning and preparation will be needed.

Care is also needed with the words we are using here. When we say 'the intentional building of relationships', we do not mean 'intentional' to be understood as the opposite of 'organic' or happening naturally. Even the strictest organic farmers and gardeners do not simply step back and let things happen. In fact they take enormous care in their preparation, but do *as little as necessary for healthy growth to occur*.

Gardeners will recognise the need to prepare the soil thoroughly before planting a delicate seedling. Much effort will be needed to ensure the soil is free of tangling weeds that would choke the seedling, that the soil is sufficiently moist and full of the correct nutrients. Once seedlings have been planted the attentive gardener will want to make sure that the right conditions continue, but ultimately the gardener will stand back, go inside and leave the seedling to do its growing.

The same is true of relationship building. We must plan for and prepare the way especially when someone's needs are complex or their behaviour is hard to understand, easy to misinterpret or perplexing to others.

What do we do as parents of typical children when we wish to intentionally build and foster friendships and relationships in their lives?

We might approach other parents to strengthen an invitation to other children to our home. We make sure that the best DVD that everyone is into is going to be played and that pizza (or another child friendly food) is going to be available. When the children arrive, do we sit with our own child as the DVD is viewed and pizza eaten? No! We back off. The preparation work has been done, the conditions set and we will only spoil things if we stay. We retreat from the room in the hope that the conditions we have created will help foster the relationships in the room. We have intentionally tried to build relationships.

None of us can ever make other people become friends with each other. But we can set favourable conditions and then see what happens.

Children and adults are routinely rejected and excluded across the UK and beyond in classrooms, playgrounds, staffrooms, work places and communities.

Colin's son Elliot, aged 10, came home in tears from school one day. He was inconsolable. This was very unusual for such a confident boy who has no labels or significant issues in his life. After much exploration out turned out that he had been 'voted off' his octagonal lunch table by his fellow lunch mates.

Where did they get this idea?
Yes – Reality TV

The world of media strengthens the negative human instinct to reject and exclude by means of reality television - such programmes as 'Big Brother' and 'The Weakest Link'. Voting off, ignoring, refusing to play and direct insults and offensive words and actions seem to abound in most informal community spaces occupied by children and adults.

Sorry - This is a two-player game!
You stink
F... off

Pretend you don't see her

It is notable to see that films such as *Shrek, The Shark Tale* and *Happy Feet* encourage and support the inclusive instinct. They are required viewing for all our developing children and young people, let alone any would be inclusionist!

Inclusion and Difference – Schools and Communities

Most schools, if not all, fall well short of reflecting the society around them. Our mainstream schools are only *partial communities* and neither welcome nor include the full breadth of the diversity outside their doors.

Posters urging pupils to respect difference are no substitute for the lively, daily experience of growing up with others who embody the huge variation inherent in the human condition. Different and even the most challenging pupils are icons of individuality and their inclusion is living evidence of diversity and what it takes for us all to get along.

"Do we want schools driven by test scores, with teachers and students pressurised to achieve in narrowly defined areas, eliminating anyone who stands in the way? Or do we want loving learning communities in which all people feel responsible for one another, understanding of diversity, and confident of their individual and collective agency? What role will our young people play in the world we envision, and how will we help them to develop the attitudes, skills, and inclinations that will make this dream a reality?"
Sapon Shevin, 2007

But it is not enough for these differences to simply be present; without dialogue they can easily be misconstrued. If we say nothing young people will inevitably come up with their own theories about difference and these will seldom be accurate or helpful.

At the time of writing this book there are 9,060 young people in the primary and secondary age range in England and Wales with a label of 'profound and multiple learning difficulty'. Of these over 82% (7,440) have no presence in their local community school and are

placed in separate special settings. Likewise, 72% (21,010) of those young people with a label of 'severe learning difficulty' are placed apart form their non-disabled peers. 30% of children with a label of 'autistic spectrum disorder' are segregated and it is probably safe to assume that these are the young people with most differences in terms of their behaviour and communication.

Note that how help is provided within a mainstream setting can exacerbate difference and be a barrier to relationships forming.

> **"Non-disabled kids need us to make their world safe as much as we need them. We need to be together. We all know that."**
> MacKeith, 2008

There are many ways of helping people to become more connected to the communities they live in:

Community

- via your own network of relationships
- via community mapping and connecting to persons and groups who share interests
- by locating and mobilising 'community guides'
- by using 'third places'
- by building an intentional circle of support
- by building 'community circles'

Begin by *listening for the story* not by expecting people to be able to tell you what they want in a direct way. Some call this listening for the story *tuning in.* It involves noticing the people and places that seem to work for the excluded person, where they seem happy, relaxed and comfortable. It might mean talking to the people who know and love the excluded young person if there are any such people still in their lives. The aim is to build up a picture of what matters to the person, what they care about; what makes them unique.

Third Places

Ray Oldenberg came up with the concept of third places in 1999. If the first place is your home, then the second place is your place of work, if you have one, and therefore the third places are community settings such as churches, pubs, coffee bars and so on.

Third Places are associations or connections between people that are based on locations. A third place becomes important in relationship building because you can become a regular at a café or bar, a place where you can get known without doing much. It is important to go at regular times, something that suits people who rely on routine. This might also be a place where you spot a community guide, someone who is very connected in his or her own community.

Reciprocity is likely to be important here; you need to think about what the guide will get out of getting involved with someone you are working with or care about. Guides don't always need to relate directly to the person you are supporting; sometimes you are just asking for their advice and knowledge, not involvement. At other times such people can create circles of support or fill a room for a community circle (see below).

Bringing up challenging children and supporting vulnerable adults is more than the work of any one person, more than one parent, more than one teacher or carer. We need to harness the capacities that exist beyond the school, home or centre building to enhance life opportunities, provide role models and a richer range of life experiences than any home or institution could ever provide.

Simply involving the elders in a community in the lives of our most troubled individuals can be a very powerful way of changing behaviour and meeting unmet emotional needs. Alternatively, radically different thinking may take place. In North East England local fishermen were successfully engaged to mentor criminalised young men who shared their interest but who would otherwise be extremely troublesome without this mentoring.

Community Guides (McKnight 1998) who are simply well connected non-professional community members can be involved by leaders to reach out to isolated parents struggling with their challenging young person. Safe, non-paid individuals know people who know people and every locality has them! Their role can be to draw together a team or circle of support from other local non-professional people. They can also be active in eliciting invitations from others who would share interests with them, for example: 'I am a friend of your sister. She said I should approach you. I have this friend who loves to sing. She has a great voice. I think you might like her in your choir'.

Community Guides know the community territory of hospitality and rejection they work with the former and work around the latter. Community building in the interests of pupils with challenging issues must start with attempts to build and rebuild relationships among local residents, local associations and local institutes.

Historically it is clear that significant community development only takes place when local people are committed to investing themselves and their people in the effort. Top down community building or even outside in tends not to work. School leaders are uniquely placed inside communities and have powerful opportunities to lead and facilitate change. Local people will unite very powerfully around shared concerns or agreed aims and this can be a very powerful force given effective leadership.

Ultimately the committed worker or practitioner will be changed by the work if it is done authentically. Relationships are dynamic, complex, nuanced and ongoing. The work is never done.

Let us consider three substantial forms of intentional relationship building that we have been pursuing and promoting over the last 10 years. We will begin with our latest.

Community Circles

The purpose of community circles is to intentionally bring people from a local community together to share their skills, talents, gifts and resources. Inspired by the work of Lois Smidt and *Beyond Welfare in Iowa* (ABCD in Action, 2006), this idea is based upon the premise that ALL of us need three things in our lives to make us happy and fulfilled: these are *money, friendship and meaning*. We believe that everyone needs community, everyone needs to be heard and everyone needs to have fun.

> **"I really enjoyed the gathering and it just highlighted what inclusion is all about. I have never seen it so brilliantly demonstrated; it was as if a veil had been lifted from my eyes."**
> Pat, Circle NG3

Beyond Welfare is a gathering of citizens with a simple but ambitious aim:

"to eliminate poverty in Story County by 2010".

Beyond Welfare define poverty much more widely than simply a lack or shortage of money and recognise that poverty of meaning and/or relationships are equally common in our communities. So when they say their aim is to eliminate poverty, they actually mean they:

> "strive to build a countywide community where all of us have enough money, healthy relationships and a sense of purpose and meaning".

Community circles are based upon reciprocity and the assumption that EVERYONE has both gifts and needs, whether these are labelled or not. The circles adopt the fundamental value of inclusion that *all means all,* no one is excluded from community circles, instead the circle members work out how to include everyone equally and safely.

A community circle is made up of participants and allies from the local community. The meeting starts with everyone sharing food and conversations. Next the group comes together in a circle so that everyone can see each other and shares what is good and new in their lives, everyone gets a turn to be listened to. "Good" and "new" breaks the habit of thinking about and reacting from what's wrong; it is an exercise of giving and receiving attention with one another and it also provides a solid foundation of strengths from which we can think about and tackle difficulties. The group is then asked the question what do they *want, need* or *have to offer.*

Community circles provide a great foundation or starting point from which to explore connections, build relationships, locate resources and share skills. These circles will be a particularly important resource for *Independent Support Brokers* and the disabled people that they work for. They provide a safe forum in which people can meet and friendships can start, a natural reservoir of people and relationships where people can be invited to offer their time and capacity. A community circle member states:

"To be successful we have to start from a belief in inclusion. A belief that we are all born 'in', that all means all. Everyone needs to belong; everyone is ready; everyone needs support; everyone can communicate; everyone can contribute. Together we're better."

Who could argue?

What Do We Mean by Community?

This definition from Peter Block (2008) is a good starting point:

"Community [...] is about the experience is belonging. We are in community each time we find a place where we belong...to belong is to be related to and a part of something. It is the opposite of thinking that wherever I am, I would be better off somewhere else...to belong to a community is to act as a creator and co-owner of that community. The work then, is to seek in our communities a wider and deeper sense of emotional ownership; it means fostering among all of a community's citizens a sense of ownership and accountability."

So it is not simply about place; it is about relationship...

So what do we at Inclusive Solutions think we have learned after almost two years of creating Community Circles?

We have learned that it is still easier to say what this sort of group ISN'T rather than define precisely what it is. However we do spend time each gathering simply exploring and building a picture of what participants value about meeting in a community circle.

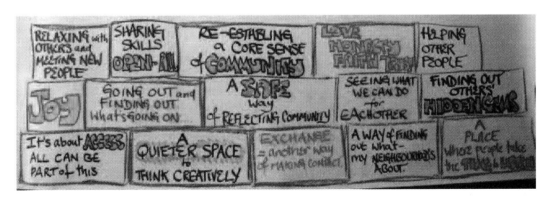

People show up (or don't) *by choice,* not because they have been referred to the community circle or had their attendance mandated by someone else.

People also need to "leave their labels at the door" (Smidt, 2009) and *come as themselves* and not in their work role or as a representative of a local service or organisation or on behalf of someone else or as a labelled person.

People will only show up if invited personally and some need a person with them to be present at all. We ensure that people are properly welcomed on arrival by assigning this role to at least three people including younger members in order to set the tone

It is about creating a context, which allows or restores what is

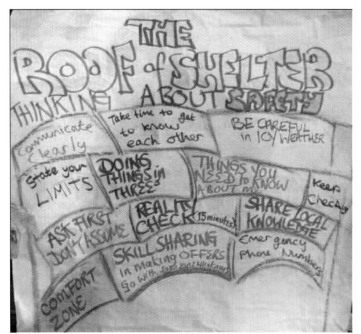

already and always there between people, namely the impulse to be generous and offer support, but, again, no one is obligated to do anything in response to a particular need, want or offer.

The safety of all needs is considered but the focus is on *natural* rather than *special* safety measures, e.g. doing things in 3s rather than 2s. It is not being vulnerable that puts you in jeopardy; it is being vulnerable *and isolated.* We asked the leadership of Beyond Welfare for their thoughts on staying safe whilst building community relatedness; this was their reply:

"...we have had many community conversations about this. We used our Thursday night gatherings to engage the community in setting the 'policy'. We have a policy that, with the little kids, at least 2 adults/care providers are present so that there is an accountability/protective structure. With the youth, yes, pairs or threes to assure the same. The reality is that people get hurt in spite of protective measures, in all kinds of situations. We opt not to do 'background checks' because they are not a community structure of protection, they are an institutional 'solution'. And – if they truly worked we would not be seeing so much abuse in foster and institutionalised care where background checks are required. So we opt for a community/relational approach. It is also our experience that even people with a history

of challenging behaviours behave better in a circle of community. Good news also is the knowledge that we have not had an abuse incident in our 12 years of building community"

People who know a lot of people are important; find your community connectors. Young people of all ages are a unifying presence within community circles.

As Peter Block says:

"It's hard to argue against the next generation"

Nurture their leadership and their impulse to be generous. The community circle is a gathering where they can participate on equal terms around real and lively issues, it's not school – no one is forcing them to be there – and in our experience they keep coming back. The young people seem to appreciate the respectful space where they can offer help as well as name their own needs. They are great at welcoming and hospitality and love eating and drinking!

"It's meant a lot to see people all helping each other"
Angus, aged 15

Gatherings need to be intentionally facilitated and hold a structure. Community Circles are not an open ended get together – someone (or more than one person) leads and moves the gathering on to the next step (and finishes on time). Leadership convenes and holds the space and introduces the conversations that will happen at the gathering.

It's about the *little words* that we all understand - needs, wants, offers, hope, trust, feeling safe. Keep the gathering jargon and acronym-free. Words like 'assessment', 'safeguarding', 'collaboration' and the rest, have no place in this space.

People will come and go, show up once and not again or not regularly. Hospitality/Food – offered at the start of the gathering and available throughout suggest welcome and connection.

What happens at the end in the flurry of conversations and connections before people leave may be as important as the main meeting itself'.

Reciprocal generosity is tangible.

April, a woman with autism, sums up this kind of gathering really well:

> **'It is a meeting which is free with food and drink and where able and disabled people come together completely equally and help each other in all sorts of little and big ways [...] this meets one of the greatest needs of the disabled person to be able to help and to give. Also in the meeting is a chance to share in two's good things and needs in a respectful way."**

Circle of Friends

"It's no use giving up!"

This insightful comment comes from a Year 5 pupil who has been part of a *circle of friends* support network, for Darren, a fellow pupil in his class. Darren had shown distressed and difficult to manage behaviour throughout his school career. Over the past term a group of eight pupils from Darren's class have been brought together (with the help of their class teacher and school educational psychologist) to give time and thought to how they can be supportive towards him in the things they do and let him know that they care about who and how he is. For his part Darren has responded by doing less of the things he used to: refusing to work; running out of school and hiding; "calling" other pupils; becoming tearful at "slight" provocations that had previously made him so challenging for pupils and staff to live with. All these things had led to involvement with an Educational Psychology Service.

Intentionally building relationships through creating circles of friends (Newton and Wilson, 2005) is one approach to meeting emotional and behavioural needs. This is also a powerful way of strengthening the sense of belonging for a pupil with complex additional support needs. In this process the child's peer group can become a source of support and constructive relationship.

The rationale behind the circle of friends approach is a simple one and, once understood, almost embarrassingly obvious. It recognises that a significant consequence for someone who shows distressed and difficult behaviour is their likely isolation from their peer group both in and out of school. Teachers will describe such pupils as " having no friends", "unable to make or sustain relationships", "always fighting or arguing with other pupils". Pupils will describe them as "a nutter", "mad", "always getting done for something" although when encouraged they are able to give much more balanced descriptions.

When this kind of situation is viewed systemically and with an awareness of the powerful processes of circular causation (Dowling and Osbourne 1985, Miller 1994) it is easy to see how increasing isolation from your peer group can lead to increasing despair and bad feelings about yourself which are then reflected in your behaviour. Once you internalise the message that nobody likes you or wants to be your friend, or feel that they think you are mad, feel that they will do things just to wind you up, it is easy to conclude that you have nothing to lose by giving full vent to your feelings and distress in the way you behave. And when you do, the subsequent behaviour of your classmates simply confirms your worst fears about yourself and how others see you. Thus is created a very vicious circle in which the effects of your behaviour have become the subsequent causes of your behaviour.

The people around you and their interventions may accelerate this process. You may find yourself on the receiving end of a behaviour programme, which is founded on ignoring difficult behaviour in case it is reinforced by the reward of attention. (How we came to believe that there could be anything helpful or therapeutic in being ignored by others suggests further study.)

You may not have qualified for a "programme" as such but it is very likely that the message given to the rest of the class by the adults around you will be along the lines of "don't get involved, it's not your business, just ignore him". You may find yourself in time out or isolation and although this may be helpful in letting you save face and in limiting your public image it is unlikely in itself to address the unmet needs that are fuelling your behaviour.

The circle of friends approach (Newton and Wilson, 2005) is at the opposite and more restorative end of the continuum of interventions from approaches based on ignoring difficult behaviour. It is a systemic approach that recognises the power of the peer group (and thereby of pupil culture) to be a positive as well as a constraining or exacerbating influence on individual behaviour.

If we accept that peer group isolation can worsen things for an individual then it follows that efforts to increase that individual's inclusion within his peer group are likely to help that same individual. If circles can be vicious they can also be virtuous if efforts are made to set and maintain a context for this. For schools the resource implication of this approach is minimal and this is because the key resources, i.e. other pupils, are always and already there. Adult time is however needed both to mobilise the friendship

circle and to facilitate its problem solving skills as the circle develops.

This is still a relatively new approach to working with emotional and behavioural difficulties within UK schools, but has been used in parts of North America and Canada for a number of years to promote the inclusion of disabled pupils in mainstream schools (Pearpoint and Forrest 1989). Within the North American work the circle of friends approach is used as one means of normalising the life experiences of disabled pupils who are recognised as vulnerable to isolation from the ordinary pattern of extended relationships and friendships. Such isolation is seen as a risk associated with a system of segregated schooling where students' opportunities to know and be known by the wider peer group in their community are limited by their institutional and often geographical separation. This impoverishment of the breadth of relationships that people who are not disabled and segregated would take for granted, remains a major and uncounted cost of any system of separate special school education (Gold 1994).

In terms of support initiatives currently in use in the UK, the circle of friends approach has links with the "No Blame" approach to bullying described by Barbara Maines and George Robinson. This approach looks to pupils themselves for their solutions to episodes of bullying. There are also links with work taking place at Acland Burghley Comprehensive School in London and elsewhere to train anti-bullying counsellors. Here pupils in Year 8 and above have been trained in basic counselling skills to enable them to offer support to other pupils who are experiencing bullying. The circle of friends approach also sits comfortably with many of the declared aims of the typical Personal and Social Education curriculum, the primary and secondary SEAL strategy and Restorative Justice initiatives (see below). The common ethos of these approaches lies in staff sharing responsibility for problem solving with pupils.

We have found that this work radically challenges so many of our core constructs about how we operate as professionals. We have welcomed a fresh approach to speaking openly about feelings, vulnerabilities, emotions and behaviour with children and adults. We have appreciated the inclusive drive of the work and its challenge to segregation and exclusion. We feel we are working here with an approach which strengthens the individual's place in the community without the trappings of a within child model focusing on what is wrong with a pupil - their deficits. The approach is systemic but involves the individual and their peers. We enter the messy world of human relationships but without the curse of feeling

artificial or that we are engaged in social engineering. We are authentically, impacting on behaviour but are not being controlling adult behaviourists. Perhaps the circle of friends model is the antidote to so much social skills training and assertive discipline style approaches to behaviour management which have left so many of us feeling cold and had so little impact on the most vulnerable individuals in our society.

The ideas implicit in the approach lend themselves to so many situations. Why should not every child in a special school have their own circle of friends in their local mainstream school? Every new entrant to a school who has had prior problems would surely benefit. Any disabled pupil isolated by the reactions and behaviour of others around them would surely benefit if nothing else could be employed to create conducive conditions for friendship?

This is not a lightweight strategy and many would argue that inclusion has to be wholesale cultural change. In a school it should be everyone's business not just a team of volunteer pupils. Circle time and other strategies could be more mainstream routes to encouraging acceptance and celebration of diversity. But if nothing is working, in our experience, build a team!

Circles of Support

Circle of support is the term generally used for circles that have been created around disabled adults or children in the community. Sometimes families in their own homes have created these. Circles are created around a person by purposeful invitation. This *inviting* is best carried out not by a direct family member but by someone who is prepared to support or advocate on behalf of the individual. Shared interests or motivation can sometimes be used as a way of growing circles together.

When a circle is created someone needs to facilitate the circle meetings on a regular basis. The circle can be located in a person's home or in a neutral venue guided by their choice. Often circles will have people of a range of ages present. As ever diversity will be the strength of an effective circle. There will always be energy around trying to increase opportunities for more time in ordinary places, friendship opportunities and meaningful activities.

A typical agenda for early meetings of such circles is likely to include the following five:

- Welcome, food and drink

- Person's dreams
- Person's interests
- What can circle members do to help the person reach towards dreams and engage in interests in ordinary places with ordinary people
- Closing reflections

Restorative Interventions

A third way we can work intentionally around relationships is when things are at their worst and may be about to break; when harm has been caused. We need new ways to restore relationships when someone has been harmed. The space between people is where we need to focus rather than being preoccupied with punitive consequences for the wrongdoer.

"Bad behaviour in our schools, often leading to school exclusions, speeding the pupils involved to the social scrapheap, has become a blight on our education system. Solutions are hard to come by. Most come in the form of yet more punitive discipline, which merely heightens the problem. What is needed in schools is fresh thinking, new approaches that work - and Restorative Practices are precisely that. Restorative Practices break the cycle by tackling the root causes of misbehaviour, rather than just massaging the symptoms. Many badly behaved pupils, faced directly and personally with the harm they have done to others, not only see the error of their ways but are often even transformed into positive role models. And they don't need to be excluded."
Sir Charles Pollard, ex-Chief Superintendent, Thames Valley Police, 2008.

For fuller exploration and practical detail as well as theoretical and research findings around this whole area of restorative interventions and justice see Mahaffey and Newton (2008).

Restorative interventions:

- Seek to safely include all those affected by an incident in its resolution.

- Seek to facilitate an understanding of each other, helping resolve conflict and repair harm.

Inclusive
Solutions

- Take account of the views of the victim and challenge the behaviour of the offender.

- Give the offender the opportunity to make amends.

- Separate the deed from the person, thus removing much of the punitive element from the process.

New ways of thinking about behaviour and relationships with children and young people should pave the way in the longer term for a more peaceful world. Our young people need new ways of relating to each other, new ways of making accommodations to the challenges that human relationships pose and, most of all, new ways of handling conflicts that do not lead to increasing escalation, punitive approaches, bullying or violence.

Whilst most of our experience has been in schools the principles and processes of restorative interventions are very relevant to adults with challenging behaviour who also have labels arising from mental health or disability. Many adults with severe reputations and highly challenging behaviour are dealt with in simplistic behavioural processes involving punishments and rewards with little attention being paid to relationship, love, forgiveness or restoration when harm occurs. This needs to change.

> **"Restorative Justice is a process by whereby all the parties with a stake in a particular offence come together to resolve collectively how to deal with the aftermath of the offence and it's implications for the future"**
> Graef, 2001

Restorative Justice aims to restore the balance of a situation disturbed by a crime or conflict and make good the harm caused to the individuals concerned. Restorative interventions provide a fair process; any outcome must be seen to be just by both parties. The process is positive in its frame and places great emphasis on how things will be in the future. Restoration stresses the importance of relationships over rules. Such processes seek at all times to restore the relationships damaged by harmful or offensive behaviours.

Punishment and control simply do not work. Their impact is limited in terms of changing undesired behaviours, addressing conflict in complex relationships or in creating a more harmonious, collaborative environment.

"Retribution is a familiar concept in relation to punishment, encapsulated in such sayings as 'an eye for an eye' and 'getting their just desserts ' Sentences are arrived at according to the relevant categories of offence, and in relation to other, similar cases, so that fairness is assured, and justice is seen to be done. Offences are deemed to be offences against the state, and it is the state that is responsible for sentencing and punishment, according to law."
Drewery, 2004.

In contrast, restorative solutions focus on the social and emotional impact of offences and are:

"...preoccupied with processes that will not only redress the effect of the offence on the victim, but will also restore the situation, including the damage done to relationships, and even to offenders themselves.
In this paradigm, wrongdoing is seen as primarily a violation of people and of relationships. The focus is on the harmful effects of offending. Offenders are required to meet those affected, to take responsibility for their actions, and to make amends. A major feature of the approach is that it brings together a community of care around both the offender and those affected, and both 'sides' share in the resolution of the problem."
Drewery, 2004.

What is Restorative Justice?

Traditionally, conferencing in the UK has been associated with *family group conferencing* (Zehr, 2003) which involves the young person, family members, supporters of the victim and his/her family and supporters and possibly other community members.

In a school context there can be *small/short conferences* involving pupils only and *full conferences* involving pupils, parents/ carers. Full conferences may include any relevant parties and supporters even including community members. These are for more serious occurrences and may relate to things that have extended to problems outside school.

The common thread in both small and large conferences is the fact that each follows broadly the same structure and format. There is a formality about them with a focus on resolution with the agreements coming from the children themselves. Follow-up is also an important part of the process.

Conferencing is thus a way of bringing two or more people together to address wrongdoing and conflict. All participants are encouraged to speak and express their feelings. All participants have a say in the outcome.

Key elements of a restorative conference:

- It is **voluntary**- everyone is there by choice (informed)
- It **brings together** the participants
- The starting position of the facilitator is one of **appreciation** of the choice that everyone has made to be there
- It creates a **safe** and **supportive** environment,
- It keeps the process **focused** and records the decisions of the group/pupils
- The conference facilitator does not make or influence the decisions
- All participants are **encouraged** to **express** themselves and to find their own **creative solutions**
- The **participants** involved are there because they are those **directly affected** by what has happened.

Restorative solutions take many forms in schools and care settings. Some can be done routinely, others will take time, commitment and planning to fully implement. Each process can directly involve other pupils/young people in lead roles. Some are more directly focused on restorative outcomes than others.

The three levels at which **restorative interventions** can take place are:

1. Day to day use of restorative language
2. Small/Short conferences
3. Full/Large conferences

Many readers will feel that they already work restoratively and indeed much excellent practice in schools designed to develop personal, social skills and relationships will be restorative.

Working restoratively is participatory. It is an approach that sees misbehaviour as essentially a violation of people and relationships rather than a violation of rules or establishments or organisations. Restorative justice, in its widest sense, is defined as "all those affected by an incident or conflict being involved in finding a

Three Levels of Restorative Interventions

mutually acceptable way forward". Wrong doers are also recognised as having been affected and therefore involved in finding the way forward. The various processes that can be used to repair harm demand certain skills of facilitators. These include active, empathic listening, impartiality and an ability to empower others to come up with their own solutions to problems (Robin Tinker 2006).

Bullied by a Gang

Helen was a Year 10 girl in an inner city comprehensive. Small for her age, she had been teased and bullied about her appearance for many years but the problem reached a new intensity when she was surrounded by a gang of eight girls in the school yard and subjected to ten minutes of constant haranguing and taunting. Teachers witnessed the incident and stopped the girls. After talking to Helen, they finally realised the extent of the problem. Various strategies had been tried over the years but nothing had really worked.

Restorative approaches had just been introduced into the school, and Helen's head of year decided to try to resolve the situation by setting up some meetings run on restorative lines. However, Helen was unwilling to meet face to face with her eight tormentors, even though she desperately wanted the bullying to stop. Her head of year managed to arrange eight separate meetings where the themes that had been identified in that had been identified in Helen's thoughts and feelings were addressed with each child at the appropriate points.

Each one had a different experience and perspective. The responsibility of the facilitator was to ensure that there was a detailed account of the event itself, the thoughts and feelings of those whose actions caused the harm and also how Helen experienced it. This proved to add to the effective experience of the event with the context being set for each individual, which in turn helped them to relate their side of the story and the impact of their actions on Helen. To varying degrees, the eight girls were shocked at how Helen felt about what they had thought was a harmless game. Most of them volunteered to become her friend, while the others said that they would leave her alone. Helen's last three terms at school were her happiest, and she ended up gaining some creditable GCSE results and enrolling in the local FE college.

A short restorative conference usually involves at least three people: the adult who is dealing with the incident and the two children or young people involved. Each participant is encouraged to tell what has happened, what they were thinking and feeling at the time, who was affected by the incident and then the harm that has been done is identified. Each is invited to say what they think should be done to repair the harm or make things right. This approach is suitable for most minor incidents, conflicts and disputes where parents/carers do not need to be involved. These short conferences can sometimes be run at short notice and on the spot preferably in a quiet room without a table and with chairs placed in a circle without a table as a barrier. We have been pressed to run short conferences during lesson time in quiet parts of the dining hall, in the library or in unused classrooms but this is far from ideal, as there are always distractions and potential interruptions.

The Conference Format
(Tinker et al, 2006.)

This is a basic conference format. Similar questions are asked to each person present to ensure fairness. Given the different positions held there will be a slight variation in the questions asked of each participant and you will need to trust your instincts and sensitivity to judge when and how to do this. Be flexible.

1. Introductions: introduce whoever is present.

2. Welcome: thank both pupils for coming and stress that they have <u>agreed</u> to come. To show appreciation that they have begun the process and want things to be different, it is appropriate to congratulate individuals for choosing to attend. In some settings such as the Hammersmith and Fulham pilot schools, children and young people prefer to include a few basic ground rules at the beginning of the conference and this option will be discussed further in the next chapter.

   The facilitator needs to appear neutral, but warm and encouraging as they open up this meeting. The situation needs to be safe and well managed. A certain business like professionalism needs to be clear in the demeanour of the facilitator from the outset. The meeting **is** going to be effectively chaired.

3. State the purpose of the conference, for example:

"We are here today to focus on the incident which happened on ____ between **A** *(person who harmed) and* **B** *(person harmed).* **A** *has admitted his/her part in the incident. We are not here today to take sides or decide who is right or wrong or good or bad but to look in detail at what happened and how* **B** *was affected by that. We will look into how harm can be repaired and hopefully draw up an agreement together, which will set out how things can be put right. Both of you will have the opportunity to have your say and be listened to. I will be asking you questions in turn."*

This may have to be reworded for some people. The facilitator needs to ensure that all present have understood what has been said. The facilitator must take care to avoid any suggestion of blame, judgement, or anger in their nonverbal communications as well as in what they are saying aloud.

4. *Questions to* **A**:

What happened?
What were you thinking?
How did you feel?
What have your thoughts been since that time?
Who has been affected by your actions?

5. *Questions to* **B**:

What happened?
What were you thinking?
How did you feel?
What has been the hardest thing for you?
Who else has been affected by what happened?

6. *Question to* **A**:

You have just heard how **B** *has been affected by what you did and how what you did has caused harm. Is there anything you would like to say?*

A's response:...

Inclusive
Solutions

Alternatively in the case where both parties have been responsible for causing harm to the other we might say to **A** and **B**:

We have heard what each of you have to say; tell me what you are feeling now?

7. Question to **A:**

What can you do to put things right?

Variations to this question:

What do you need (is there anything you can do) to do to put things right? Is there anything more you want to say?

8. **A** offers reparation.

Offering reparation is difficult for some children and young people. Allow them time to come up with something. If the facilitator judges that the child or young person is really struggling, he or she may wish to invite some ideas from the other young person or to ask a question like: *What do you think **B** might need in order to feel safe with you?* Tentatively offering some ideas and suggestions may be appropriate for those children who continue to struggle; ensure that a range of options is offered. Also it is crucial that you ensure that the chosen options have some meaning to **A**. The young person can then translate these into their own words and say how they will carry them out i.e. days, times etcetera. What is offered must be realistic and achievable.

The facilitator could ask further questions to find out who might be able to support and assist the young person in honouring the commitment. A useful question at this stage might be: *Is there anyone else who can support you in this?*

9. Question to **B**:

How do you feel about that offer?

10.   Question to **A**:

On (date) you made the choice to (summarise the incident) and today you have made another choice and have agreed to (summarise reparation offered). Which choice do you feel better about?

11.   Question to **B**:

*You have heard **A** say how his/her behaviour has caused harm and what he/she will do to put this right. How do you feel now?*

12.   Pupils draw up the agreement.

- Both sign it
- Agree to meet again to review how things are going and whether the Agreement has been adhered to in a reconvened conference.
- Date this.

The process of completing the agreement and signing can be a time of informal reconnecting for the involved pupils. The facilitator is wise to give them some space as they do this.

13.   Questions to **A**:

You have said that you have taken responsibility for what you did and that you are going to put things right by: (sum up agreement) How do you <u>feel</u> now?
How will (these people) feel if you do not keep to the agreement?
How will s/he feel if you keep to the agreement?
How will you feel if you keep to the agreement?

At this stage you might want to say something about the

follow up meeting and the form that will take. Sometimes this might be informal but for more serious cases setting a time to check how the agreements are going is important.

14.   Facilitator congratulates **A** and **B** on making positive choices and both for listening to each other. Emphasise **B**'s courage for facing **A.**

Thank pupils for coming.

Post Conference tasks:

• Staff information sheet completed and posted on notice board

• Conference record sheet completed - Copies in each pupil's files

• Agreements photocopied - originals to pupils - copy to each pupil's file

Evaluation sheets (if used) – a copy for **A** and **B** and copies for school staff involved.

We are reaching for the possibility of *forgiveness* in this new restorative language of relationships. This is the new, but ancient 'f' word. We reach here for a timeless value. Forgiveness can be requested and can be offered. Our every day language needs to embrace this strong restorative concept. Can you picture adults forgiving each other publicly, adults asking pupils to forgive them and actively forgiving pupils? This is the challenge.

Forgiveness

> **"Forgiveness does not mean ignoring what has been done or putting a false label on an evil act. It means, rather, that the evil act no longer remains as a barrier to the relationship. Forgiveness is a catalyst creating the atmosphere necessary for a fresh start and a new beginning. It is the lifting of a burden or the cancelling of a debt."**
> Martin Luther King, 1963

The three approaches outlined above share the following principles:

- Intentionality

- Inclusiveness

- Expecting the best

- Tapping into an existing mainstream peer group

- Listening beneath words and actions

- Participation

- Hopefulness

- Focusing on capacity rather than impairment

- Restoration

- Actively engaging people of all ages in solutions

Practical Implications

- Reflect on your own community and those you have relationships with

- Consider where you need to build relationships for those you work with or care about

- Identify intentional relationship building strategy that will fit your situation

- Implement approach and see what you learn

Hard Questions

- What do you do if someone does not want to leave their home even though they are isolated?

- If someone is distressed but refuses to work with you to build relationships in their life what should you do?

- Are friendships essential for everyone?

- Is community essential to inclusion?

- What should we do with someone who continues to cause extreme harm to those he is close to?

Resources

- Tinker, R. (2005). *Restorative Justice Handbook*. Nottingham City/Inclusive Solutions.

- Newton, C. and Wilson, D., (2005) *Creating Circles of Friends*, Inclusive Solutions.

- Newton, C. and Wilson, D., (2006) *Circles of Adults,* Inclusive Solutions.

- Mahaffey, H and Newton C. (2008) *Restorative Solutions.* Inclusive Solutions.

The Seventh Key: Gifts – Focus on Capacity

> **"Our gift is who we are."**
> MacKeith, 2009

"Is the glass half empty or half full? is a common expression, used rhetorically to indicate that a particular situation could be a cause for optimism (half full) or pessimism (half empty); or as a general litmus test to simply determine if an individual is an optimist or a pessimist. The purpose of the question is to demonstrate that the situation may be seen in different ways depending on one's point of view and that there may be opportunity in the situation as well as trouble. This idiom is used to explain how people perceive on events and objects. Perception is unique to every individual and is simply one's interpretation of reality." (Wikipedia, 2009.)

Ask the same question of someone who is different, disabled, challenging or for whatever reason needs additional support and the question becomes even more profound. Difference and challenge appear to evoke more pessimistic responses:

What's wrong with that person?

Is there a label?

What's their problem?

Is there a cure?

This is the dominant *deficit* view of children and adults who are different or challenging. *What is wrong with them*? This is the dominant medical model that haunts the thinking of so many professionals and families across the world. This medical mindset even dominates the thinking of lead practitioners working in education and social care.

We argue that is much more socially and educationally productive to focus on a child or adult's capacity not their shortcomings or difficulties. Gifts not deficits. Strengths not weaknesses.

To do this we will need fire, wind and some dramatic attitude and mindset changes!

Diagnoses, Labels and the Myth of Explanation

We are trapped by the myths that have been created around the explanatory power of labels like 'autism' or 'learning difficulties'. All of us have been taught that there is a thing called autism (the child 'has' autism), a thing called 'learning difficulties' and so on. We then think that this thing explains and defines the behaviours that are associated with it. All that has really been created here is a disturbing non sequitur. Here's how it works in the case of autism. Parents take their child to a paediatrician because they are concerned about his unusual and hard to understand behaviours: he rocks and spins things and he can't talk but he does echo what is said to him sometimes. After taking some further case history the paediatrician says: 'your child has autism'.

That is usually it. But imagine if those parents went back to the paediatrician to ask 'But *why* does he rock, spin and echo?' The answer would be: 'Because he has autism'.

And how do we know that? The paediatrician may say we know it because he rocks, spins and echoes... and so we've come round in an empty explanatory circle. There is only a tiny amount of caricature in the above scenario and the implications for the people labelled with this kind of self-cancelling stamp are serious and carry a life sentence. People with this label are now at huge risk of being looked at as if they were very different from the rest of us. The label becomes reality for them and us and thus we forget that we only have a poor understanding of why people with the label of autism do the things they do. Another way of putting this is: people do things for a reason and the reason isn't autism. Ultimately it's about expanding our definition of what it means to be human.

> **"We have to start being honest and humble about the fact that we are very limited in our ability to assess people with severe communication difficulties. Instead of getting better and better at knowing them with our tests and checklists we may be merely getting better and better at agreeing with one another"**
> Anne Donnellan, 1999

Social and Medical Models

The medical model focuses on an individual's impairment and assumes it is the mental or physical impairment that causes their disability. Medical professionals who are trained to reduce the effects of such impairments see disability as a medical problem and hold the belief that removal of the impairment will result in success in curing the disability. The degree of disability in the medical model is quantified and the severity assessed to be on how much an individual deviates from a typical population norm.

This model reflects a belief that human beings are malleable and alterable whilst society is fixed and unalterable thereby suggesting that it is the responsibility of a disabled person to adapt to a hostile environment (Rieser and Mason, 1992).

The medical model is highly influential and affects policy, practice and attitudes of many professionals and families.

The medical model does not consider disabled people's views or capacities. Whilst many have medical conditions that may or may not require treatment, disabled people can live enriched lives.

Disabled people believe that it is society's barriers to people with impairments accessing the world that causes disability not the impairments themselves. This is known as the *Social Model of Disability* (Rieser and Mason, 1992)

A social model framework views disability as a social construct. Impaired individuals unable to conform with society's norms often feel oppressed and discriminated against. The social model suggests that rather than requiring people who have an impairment to change, social and cultural norms must change. Social model goals could work on a wide scale and encapsulate the struggle of other oppressed groups therefore providing a better world to live in. (Rieser and Mason, 1992)

The social model challenges the existence of special education. Excluding or segregating people who have impairments is diminishing to both disabled and able-bodied people alike (Ash, 1997).

The changes implied here are more than simply redecorating the kitchen. These changes will mead that the house has to be rebuilt.

For instance, in the UK the formal assessment process leading to a statement of special educational needs is meant to be an educational decision-making process that involves a range of professionals and families in determining what provision should be made for a child with

complex needs. However anyone looking at the completed document will get a strong sense of the medical model at work as they read lists of difficulties and needs with recommended provision and placement to address these. Statements of school need not pupil need would be a start...

The social model may not actually go far enough in addressing the radical changes needed to the way we think about and work with children and adults who are different. To genuinely focus on contribution and capacity in all children and adults will require nothing less than a major paradigm shift. Perhaps we need a *contribution and relationship* paradigm? Let us consider further contribution made by different and challenging children and adults. To do this we must move to Chicago and respect the work of Professor John McKnight.

Half Full?

"Every single person has capabilities, abilities and gifts. Living a good life depends on whether those capabilities can be used, abilities expressed and gifts given. If they are, the person will be valued, feel powerful and well-connected to the people around them. And the community around the person will be more powerful because of the contribution the person is making."
Kretzman and McKnight, 1993.

Kretzman and McKnight create the connection between intentionally building relationships and community and the importance of focusing on gifts. Everyone has a gift if we choose to focus on it.

Getting Beyond the Label

Many of us have complex job titles. These titles may be very grand and conceal the humanity that hides behind.

When training groups of professionals we like to carry out the following activity:

We select a member of the group who has a long job title. We invite the group using only their knowledge of the person's job title to select some birthday presents for the individual. We then ask the individual to rate these presents out of 10. Usually the score is below five.

Next, we ask the person what their interests are. Using this information we invite the group to reselect a birthday present for the

individual. Again we ask them to rate the birthday present and usually the score is around 10.

The simple point behind this activity, which we learnt from Carol Tashie of New Hampshire, is that we will always do better when we know what someone brings, than we will ever do from just a person's label.

The same can be said of any child or adult with a diagnostic label. Consider someone you know who carries such a label. Set out a pie diagram in which each slice represents a part of that person. Do not forget to include their relationships. Maybe he is a son, a brother and a friend to someone?

Notice as you lay out the slices of the pie how that part that represents their label e.g. autism, falls into perspective.

The Pie or Pizza Approach

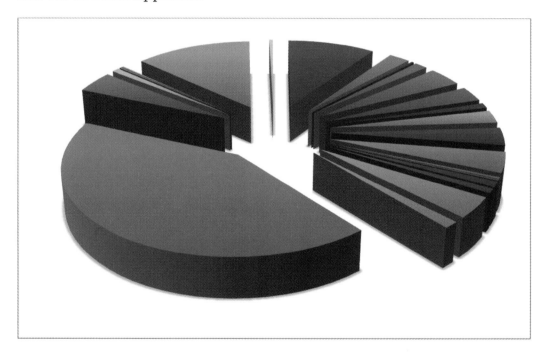

Any visiting "expert" can spot a child's or adult's difficulties or problems. It takes someone who is very familiar with a child to know their relationships, strengths, gifts and talents. Thus family members, teaching assistants and other frontline staff are often best placed to provide information on capacity. Part of a new paradigm for *contribution and relationships* would be a new respect for gift spotters and talent touts. In fact professional training would be all about noticing contribution and capacity and much less on identifying and assessing deficits and difficulties.

Once such strengths had been elicited these would feed directly into individual and group planning in an unprecedented way.

Such positive information is rich for those planning educational and social interventions and opportunities for children and adults:

"Now we know what to build on."

Jonathon, Dragon Dictate

"Jonathon is one of our biggest success stories. He has very challenging behaviour and has a statement for behavioural difficulties. Papers were sent to several special schools in the country but he wasn't accepted by them. So we decided that rather than permanently exclude him which is where we had almost got to we would have to do some radical rethinking to keep him in school. He has remarkable aptitude in a number of subjects which include ICT. So we asked him to join with the teaching staff and learning support staff on the training for Dragon Dictate and then asked him to work with individual pupils with disabilities to train them up. He has been absolutely delighted and it has built his self-esteem up. But he has also been very,very good with the students and has had many very good successes with them working with them on that programme."

Deputy Head, Helen Kenward (Channel 4 Video).

Helen and her team appear to instinctively get this new way of thinking. Take particular note of the way in which in the face of a very negative situation in which permanent exclusion seems the only option the team moved to *radical rethinking.* This captures the spirit of the new inclusive paradigm to which we are alluding.

If you always do what you've always done you always get what you've always got.

The team's response to Jonathan was indeed radical. They set him on a staff INSET day and they set him up to work with some of their most vulnerable students. They recognised his ICT skills and his capacity to contribute and work altruistically with others.

Judith Snow – the gifts of people with unusual bodies and what those vulnerable to rejection bring to community?

We were lucky to hear Judith speaking in 2002 about the gifts of people with unusual bodies. She also spoke at a conference in 2004 about the gifts of those at greatest risk of rejection and exclusion in our societies. Judith herself is a disabled woman with complex impairments and very little independent movement. Listen to the radical points she makes about these gifts:

Hospitality
- Making people feel happy
- Listening
- Providing a home to a tenant, companion or personal assistant

Grounding
- Slowing people down, reorienting people to time and space
- Leading people to appreciate the simple things
- Causing people to appreciate their own abilities

Skill Building
- Pushing people to be better problem solvers
- Causing people to try things have never done before
- Causing people to research things they never encountered before
- Improving education
- Improving technology

Networking
- Reaching out to people and breaking down barriers
- Asking questions that everyone else is too shy to ask
- Bringing people together who otherwise would never meet

Economic
- Providing jobs to people who want supplemental income like students and artists
- Providing jobs to people who need to work on schedules like home makers
- Providing jobs to people who otherwise have few or no marketable skills
- Filling odd niches

Emotional and Spiritual
- Often model exemplary forgiveness
- Offering opportunities to do something that clearly makes a difference
- Reorienting values from accumulation to relationships

Linked to Judith's last point: we often ask groups of educators to consider Christopher Reeves, the actor who had played Superman; when he fell off his horse and became paralysed for the rest of his life from the neck down, what was most important to him? How much money he had? Or was it who would stay in relationship with him, who would bathe him, who would love him? Who would support him in his battles with the system.

Judith indeed challenges our thinking She reminds us how powerful focusing on gifts can be. She neatly flips over traditional concepts of charity, doing things for disabled people, 'wonderful us, poor them' constructs.   She reminds us that disabled people themselves are delivering the goods whether we recognise this or not. Their contribution when we choose to focus on this is enormous.

Paula Kluth encourages us to use gifts and strengths in very practical ways in classrooms and communities.   Read on to consider the practical utility of focusing on *strengths and strategies.*

Getting Practical

What Are Strength and Strategies Pages?
Strength & strategies pages are simply lists that provide positive and useful information about a single learner. One list contains a student's strengths, interests, gifts, and talents. The other list answers the question, "What works for this student?" This list should contain strategies for motivating, supporting, encouraging, helping, teaching, and connecting with the learner.

When Do I Use Strengths and Strategies Pages?
Strengths and strategies pages can be used anytime for any purpose. I often use them to begin IEP meetings. They can also be used as an attachment to a positive behavior plan or as a communication tool for teams who are transitioning a student from teacher to teacher or school to school.

Why Use Strengths and Strategies Pages?

While this tool is not complex and does not necessarily provide a team with new information, it can help teachers organise the information they have and understand it in a new way. The focus on positive language and capacities can prompt educators to think and talk about students in more proactive way. It can also help teachers make changes in their planning and in their daily practice. Specifically, educators may be able to use these forms to:

- plan curriculum and instruction
- create curricular adaptations
- develop student goals and objectives
- design supports for challenging situations
- work more collaboratively with and elicit concrete ideas from families, and
- collaborate and communicate with each other.

Paula's work takes the paradigm of *contribution and relationship* right into the classroom in a very practical way. Let us stay in the classroom as we consider the contributions that an individual pupil can make even when they seem to bring and do nothing due to the complexity of their impairments. Daniel is the perfect example.

Daniel

We've learned a lot about this way of thinking from a little boy called Daniel. When we first met Daniel it appeared that he could do very little. His label was *profound and multiple learning difficulties*. Many thought that he should be placed in the local special school, in the special care unit. Working with a very inclusive head teacher and his loving foster parents Daniel was placed at his local mainstream school in Nottingham City, UK.

In this setting the other children became ideal gift spotters. They quickly ascertained that he did have a way of communicating "yes" and "no" involving eye blinking something that no adult had recognised. Daniel appeared to have the gift of bringing people together around him to plan to meet his needs as they worked to provide an enriching curriculum and social experience for him. One of his greatest contributions was to the other children. Daniel needed to be well stimulated to stay awake. Boring assemblies quickly became a thing of the past. The teachers were particularly challenged to keep him awake in assemblies by making these much more interactive and interesting than in the past. The children became very creative and expressive as they read to him to keep him stimulated.

"I think the main thing for me was what he taught us what his special gifts were. He taught us about profound disability. He taught us to think divergently to determine his needs, address those needs and to enable him to develop his own personality. These are things we were able to take forward when we had another child with similar disabilities. He taught us about epilepsy in a way no other child could have done or that first aid could either. He taught us not to be frightened. He taught us not to treat him as a 'sick child'. He wasn't fragile.

His special gifts were too numerous to detail. He was the most popular child in the school at the time. He was <u>loved</u> by all the children. He was invited to all their birthday parties and always went. He instilled in them compassion and care and joy. He loved to listen to stories and children loved to read to him. He couldn't speak and was never able to say they had read a passage wrongly. So he was the person they most wanted to practice their reading to. He loved that closeness. And that made him smile.

Perhaps my outstanding memory was one lunchtime. Just one hour before lunch, we had admitted an Irish traveller girl. Daniel sat one side of me at the dinner table and Katrina the other. She had only ever been in school for 4 days in the whole of her life and had never met a black child or a child with such disability. Katrina watched as I made a right pig's ear of trying to feed Daniel. In the end, Katrina told me to move over and said in a broad Irish accent 'Ah, give it here'. She took the spoon from me and fed him his complete dinner. No concerns about his not being able to chew, swallow or that he dribbled all over. Daniel took his food with relish. They looked like a partnership that had known each other for ever. Two children on the very edge of society brought together so perfectly and instinctively at our school dinner table.

He and his family travelled back to Nottingham for the wedding of one of his support assistants he had when with us. He was a page boy and carried the rings on a cushion on his lap."

Judy Berry, Headteacher, Rufford Infant School: Memories of Daniel, 2009

It would appear, and is perhaps no surprise, that children have no difficulty in focusing on strengths and have little interest in piles of reports or labels.

Written Reports – How Should We Document 'Special Educational Needs'?

Most written reports about people with additional needs who may be disabled, challenging or have severe reputations that appear in the medical, social or educational world share many features. Well-meaning professionals often with many years experience, write most of the reports. The reports may be well articulated, clearly laid out and even be well structured. However these reports are too often a pseudo-medical, deficit-orientated with a preoccupation with problems, weaknesses and difficulties. Strategies and solutions may be present, as part of advice and recommendations but often these may not feel meaningful to those closest to the child or adult themselves. Such reports would fall well short of person centred planning criteria, particularly the requirement to have done to you what you would do to another. Children's Services in the UK have the primary responsibility for identifying, assessing and, in some cases, formally documenting young people's special educational needs.

Most, if not all, Children's Services also declare an aspiration to increase the inclusion of disabled students and those with special educational needs within their local schools and communities. This aspiration is typically expressed within local authority inclusion policies as follows;

> **"We should therefore ensure that children and young people are educated in their local school or setting and only very rarely should that be set aside.**
> **Inclusion means that each child or young person will be part of a community that is empowered to support each child through to adulthood and be educated and supported within their local school or setting"**
> Excerpt from the Inclusion Policy of an English Shire County 2010

So perhaps the main reason for revising how we document needs and support is that the increased inclusion aspiration is reflected in how decision-making is done and that progress towards the target of more young people supported in their local schools is therefore more likely to happen.

Most of us in the population would hate to receive such reports about either our children or us. The striking omission will be any mention of gifts, capacity or strengths. At best, opening sentences will include a few positives to be followed by a more overwhelming set of the negative sentences. Most statements of special educational need would reflect this, as are many other reports for different purposes around people who are different.

What kinds of report would we write and read if there was a genuine focus on capacity? We already explored in earlier chapters the need to paint portraits rather than describe deficits about people we are writing about. Look at the example section below based on a real person and a recent report...

Helen's Gifts

Helen has many gifts. These capacities are what we should all be trying to build upon. Her are just a sample:

- **Can communicate with support from another person- a communication partner**

- **Academic capacities only recently recognised**

- **Sense of humour, beaming smile!**

- **Friendly and sociable nature. She likes to be with people**

- **Honesty about how she feels**

- **She challenges the system. We have to problem solve how to include her best in an educational world not originally designed to include all pupils**

- **World changer. By her presence, other pupils will change and benefit. They will learn about difference and diversity and should never be fazed when they work or encounter someone in their own family or community who is disabled. They will be better people for Helen's presence.**

This way of writing is surely more encouraging for all involved with the person. By starting with capacity we will always have something to build upon and draw upon. Let us embrace and develop this new paradigm of *relationship and contribution* and see where it leads.

Practical Implications

- Name and write down the gifts of the person who you find most challenging of whatever age

- Make a list of the gifts of your manager, your community and yourself

- Redesign any plans or learning programmes you are currently working with to incorporate the person's gifts, capacities and interests and consider these as starting points to support that person future development

- Throw away your tired, old plans.

Hard Questions

- Can we really focus on the capacities and gifts of dangerous criminals such as child sex offenders?

- What do we do when we can find no way of communicating with someone?

- How do we avoid the confusion of this key with developments in the UK for a much smaller group termed *gifted and talented* children?

Resources

- Kretzman, J and McKnight,J.' Building Communities form the Inside out', ACTA publications, 1993

- Dragon Dictate video clip from Channel 4 Documentary: Count Me in.

- Stephen's Book- www.inclusive-solutions.com/stephensbook.asp

- Paula Kluth and Patrick Schwarz (2008) *'Just Give Him the Whale' – 20 Ways to Use Fascinations, Areas of Expertise, and*

Strengths to Support Students with Autism' – this highly practical guidebook gives educators powerful new ways to think about students' 'obsessions' as positive teaching tools that can calm, motivate and improve learning.

The Eighth Key: Teams for Inclusion

"There is no power for change greater than a community discovering what it cares about."
Margaret Wheatley, 2002

When in Doubt Build a Team

When the going gets tough and the inclusion of a child or young person is beginning to seem extremely difficult if not impossible, many will conclude that the child should no longer be present. We would like to challenge this. Why do we move so quickly to assuming the child is in the wrong place? Surely the real question should not be 'do they belong here?' but rather: 'what team support is needed here for this to work?'

Or even more fundamental:

- who needs a team around them at this time?

- Who needs the team?

- Who is struggling with the inclusion most?

Is it the young person, their practitioner or teacher, their head teacher, setting manager, their parent or even a member of the local support services?

Whatever the answer a team may need to be built, rallied or reformed. The nature of and number of that team will depend upon the situation. Diversity of membership will most surely be important to strengthen the quality of the support and of the ideas generated. Use *radical rethinking* when creating a new team or when revitalising an existing one.

Creating effective teams for inclusion requires a courageous capacity for understanding and nurturing change both within the team and with those who the team work with.

Inclusive Solutions

Balance & Change

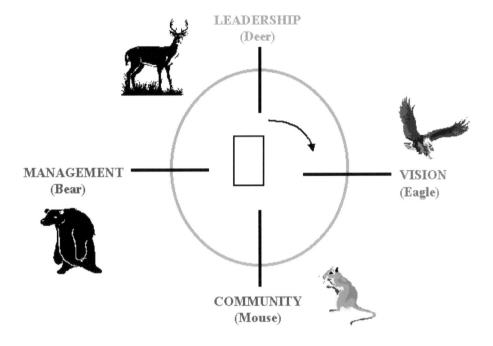

- The deer looks down from the mountain and points the direction – it opens ways to grow and evolve
- The eagle soars high and sees the whole picture below and ahead
- Mice scurry around busily together building community with warmth, friendliness and welcome
- The bear lumbers slowly but is methodical and makes things happen, the details get handled

Understanding Change: The Medicine Wheel

This is how Harrison Owen (1997), in his work on *Open Space Technology,* depicts the ancient Medicine Wheel. It is derived from centuries of tradition among First Nation Americans and is a guide to action. We have found this a powerful metaphor for understanding the process of team and organisational change and renewal.

The wheel of change begins its cycle in the north with new and **leading ideas**, with the voices that say - *'there is a better way of creating a team for inclusion'*. Travelling clockwise to the east the medicine wheel urges us to create a **shared vision** of what this team could be in our setting, school or community. Then, moving south, the wheel tells us to ask who will we need with us on the

journey. We wish to take as many **community** members along with us as we can. In an Early Years setting this would mean enrolling the support of manager, the wider staff group, parents and ultimately children. Finally, at the west, we **manage** and implement the idea. We begin to take action and turn the inclusive team into reality.

The cycle of this medicine wheel is an excellent way to think about change processes in any team, organisation or community. When we contemplate change, the risk is always that we jump prematurely from the big ideas (leadership) to how we will put these leading ideas into practice (management) and, in so doing, ignore the other two equally important points of the wheel - creating vision and engaging the wider community. The message of the medicine wheel is good work comes from keeping these four elements in balance – all are needed but none is sufficient in itself.
We must also be sure to proceed in the correct sequence.
As Harrison Owen (1997) describes it:

> **"...there is a logical sequence to the Medicine Wheel, which requires that it be circumnavigated (walked) in a clockwise direction. One begins with leadership in the north, providing the dynamism to get the show on the road. It then becomes important to ask which road and what direction. Vision supplies the answers. Once the journey is engaged, the issue is who is coming and community offers the response. Last but not least, a certain order is necessary for the journey, which is the job of management. If the elements are taken in the reverse order (counterclockwise, starting with management), the net effect is to create a marvellous organisation without ever considering who is being organised, what direction they are going in, or by what power."**

Leadership

There is a better way. Our team can be completely committed to full inclusion for all the children in our care. We will work to ensure their inclusion in our school or setting and in the surrounding community however different or challenging their additional needs may appear. When those same children leave us we will work to ensure their safe passage to the next mainstream setting, be it school, college or employment. If we have to accompany parents, or prepare the way to ensure the success of this inclusive transition, then we will do this. We will resist the voices and pressures to move

children into more segregated and special settings away from their friends and communities.

Who will we include? How about anyone who wants to attend, to participate, to be present?

All really will mean all.

There are many busy activities that any team member could engage in, but what essential or important actions will an inclusive team engage in? We need to be clear about what a team will and will not be doing. It is too easy to just add tasks to already overburdened people. Let us be clear. The work of the Nottingham City Inclusion Facilitation Team reflected in the following table illustrates what we think an inclusive team should and should not be doing:

What is Our Vision?

What Teams for inclusion should be doing	What teams for inclusion should NOT be doing
Enshrining JOINT WORKING as the team's modus operandi. Dedicating time to team building and recognising that this is a 'time hungry' but essential task. This includes building vision for their work as a team and for developments within their LEA.	Allocating patches that are the 'sole ' responsibility of the individual team member. They should not be encouraging the 'myth of the expert'.
Maintaining a focus on the learning and academic achievements of the pupils they serve.	Only be concerned with the social benefits of inclusion
Recognising that inclusion is about human rights, social justice and having insight into the disability equality issues that underpin the inclusion movement.	Focus solely on working out what is wrong with the child and identifying and meeting special needs
Using everyday language and making sense	Inventing and valuing jargon that only one person in a 1000 understands

Having high expectations. Developing an awareness of the 'unexpected benefits' of inclusion and recognising that one can be surprised.	Predicting long term limits and plateaux, inviting low aspirations and encouraging others not to expect or hope for too much from the pupils they are involved with.
Being comfortable with saying 'I don't know what to do in these circumstances but together we can work it out'. This may mean seeking out more experienced help and fresh perspectives but only where this will build on working towards your common aims.	Handing over responsibility to someone else-referring on to a higher expert and thereby opting out and perpetuating the 'myth of the expert'.
Maintaining the child's dignity by extending the range of positive, constructive and respectful metaphors with which to understand the behaviours of the children – asking 'would it be alright to do this if the child was not disabled?'	Seeking to recreate special school systems and structures in mainstream settings – e.g. establishing 'inclusion rooms'.
Promoting within team leadership by area of concern or need/recognising and valuing individual team members strengths and gifts and supporting them in becoming even better at what they already do well.	Establishing hierarchies by profession and salary/expecting all team members to be equally good at all aspects of the role.
Reaching out and empowering parents (particularly from socially disadvantaged groups) to become advocates for their child within the peer group and the wider community.	Having little or no involvement with parents of children they are supporting.

Inclusive
Solutions

Continually asking 'what is inclusion?' and developing an understanding that inclusion is a **process,** not a fixed point to be reached.	Being comfortable with and investing in the status quo. Not accepting that change is inevitable and resisting becoming active agents for change.
Identifying potential leaders for inclusion within mainstream settings and investing substantially in their development.	Allocating strictly equal shares of team time to each of the schools they serve.
Using 'only as special as necessary' as a key guide to the planning of support.	Viewing more as better. Multiple referrals create further barriers to belonging.
Working in a truly collaborative way with other services thus building true consensus in planning holistic support programmes around the child as an individual	Giving false consensus whilst believing 'we know best- we are the experts' causing tensions for the school and teacher and confusion for the child and his or her family.
Recognising and developing the role of typical peers in the inclusion process, having insights into the benefits for all.	Visit schools only to see pupils on a caseload in isolation from their peers and classes.
Believing that 'seeing it once' means its possible. Believing that pioneers lead the way for all.	Believing that if it is not statistically significant it doesn't matter – it was just a one off which cannot be repeated.
Identifying potential developments in good practice nationally and internationally and adapting these insights to our own contexts.	Thinking 'yes but it couldn't work here'.

Building on team knowledge and experience and investing in training and post-graduate study. Valuing the development of the individual team member as a vital resource.	Devoting minimal amounts of time and resources to research and professional development allowing work load to become a barrier to quality initiatives.
Working with LEAs to influence resourcing systems that do not encourage schools to rely on deficit theory but help to develop and further resourcing systems which encourage inclusive approaches.	Encouraging schools to highlight and identify difficulties as a means of securing additional resourcing.

Nottingham Inclusion Facilitation Team, 2002.

Whilst written and published eight years ago, the clear and radical direction contained above still appears fresh and relevant to those seeking to develop inter-agency and multi-professional teams today. Many emerging reorganised support services and children's centres are grappling with just these challenges.

Who Will Be Part of Teams Committed to Inclusion?

The above gives some idea of what an inclusive team might be *doing*. But what will such a team actually *look like*? We think teams who see inclusion as a central part of their work will probably not be dominated by experts but will be made up of a diverse range of practitioners with a range of skills, talents and experiences. Diversity and creativity will be their strength. A range of different thinking and learning styles will need to be present. The team will need strong leaders, influential 'people people', thinkers, system changers, reflectors, problem solvers, and deeply creative types! People of all ages and with all kinds of experiences and capacities will be pat of the core or wider team. Let us not forget those who will be there because they care passionately or those who are living daily with the experience and challenges of exclusion and inclusion.

Some people will not be comfortable with working in such a team and may need support to find a different role or to work elsewhere. Facilitative leadership and systems need to be in place for this to happen as respectfully, smoothly and as easily as possible. Whilst the work of the team is inclusion, not all will be suited to this work and we should not confuse ourselves into thinking we can include all workers in our team whatever their style, attitudes or beliefs. The stakes for including children and young people are too high for passengers or destructive practitioners. Our inclusive instincts will

want all people to be part of the future but the leadership from this team must ensure that our support to individuals does not outweigh damage to the inclusion of children. Destructive individuals can still experience belonging in another part of the world and for some, possibly away from children and families. Alternatively some individuals will need a sabbatical or a long break before they can be effective. The late, great Marsha Forest once said:

> **"I hear human service people say - I'm so tired - well leave it - get a rest. Then come back!"**
> Marsha Forrest

There is much wisdom in her words.

We will need to be systematic when we create a support team; warm and fluffy will not be enough...

'PLAN' Approach to building a team-

Support Team *(all those directly involved with a student's education)*

The key support team is made up of active agencies including family members and the whole interagency team from within school as well as those working for the student's interests outside. The questions that follow are best addressed with as many team members present as possible. By clarifying roles and responsibilities confusion, chaos, duplication, hurt feelings and dropped balls can hopefully be avoided!

- Recognise the team and clarify roles and relationships
- Develop communication system between team members for information and ideas
- Clarify who will coordinate services, information and paperwork
- Clarify who will design the teaching programme for the pupil
- Make clear who will train, plan for and support teaching assistants
- Make clear who will adapt and modify materials
- Clarify who will take care of any specialised materials
- Team members all become familiar with the student's programme

> - Share information about student specific strengths and needs, learning styles, strategies that work...See 'All about me'
> - All team members become familiar with the mainstream curriculum and with the IEP
> - What support do team members need from each other?
> - When will the team meet informally and formally

Trust

The cement that holds team members together and that at best is found between leaders and their teams is *trust*. When present this magical gel will bring out the best in any group of people, but it is so easily lost, damaged or even completely absent. A team may crumble and lose all strength and solidarity when there are trust issues present. In the social sciences, the subtleties of trust are a subject of ongoing research. In sociology and psychology the degree to which one party trusts another is a measure of belief in the honesty, benevolence and competence of the other party. It is not hard to create a checklist or even a bedside book of trust by asking any group what are the qualities of the relationship that they have with someone they truly trust. Sadly some people can trust no one but even they know what it is to *almost* trust someone. We have been asking groups about their experience of trusting relationships for the last 9 years. Below are some typical responses.

Typical qualities of trust:

- Non-Judgemental
- Honest
- Open
- Good listening
- Challenging and direct
- Always holding your best interests at heart
- Shared disclosure

Typical Behaviour around someone not trusted:

- Closed body language
- Not sharing anything personal
- Sometimes assertive or even aggressive
- Not relaxed
- Talking about the mistrusted person behind their back

Inclusive
Solutions

- Acting in an untrustworthy fashion!

Leaders do well to cultivate trust within teams. Trust will be needed if team members are to work hard on making inclusion a reality. Teams simply need trust to function at their best. Teams where trust is present and valued will also model the way for others.

Teams Visioning

"Vision without action is a daydream. Action without vision is a nightmare"
Japanese Proverb

So what would a team, truly committed to the inclusion of all children in mainstream settings, actually look like? By inviting key stakeholders and frontline practitioners to be involved in collectively visioning, a shared picture will emerge especially if the process of creating this is well facilitated.

Visioning or dreaming is about going beyond the ethos and culture that defines your school, setting or team at present.

- How would we like to see this change?
- Can we create a dream future that all can commit to?
- What value base is it rooted in?
- What blue-sky thoughts are associated with the future?

This vision or dream space is not grounded in reality but reaches for a changed world. By describing our dreams for future inclusive teams and their function we will set a clear direction. We may not reach this entire dream in our lifetimes but we may well hit key staging posts along the way. We will certainly be clear where we are heading.

Care is needed in this stage of the medicine wheel. Facilitators and leaders need to resist the temptation to create flow diagrams or

write outcomes. If they are needed they can be done later when we are in the management phase of the wheel.

Martin Luther King reached for a dream, a dream of racial equality in the United States, a dream he perhaps never thought he would see realised in his own lifetime. It was genuinely a dream and most definitely not a set of aims and objectives.

We have discovered that giving a team the opportunity to pause and reflect on what matters most to them about the work they do is a very powerful experience. The act of listening to each other creates relationship and strengthens trust and inclusion within the team; in creating a shared *vision,* groups of people build a sense of commitment together.

"I was totally blown away, when I realised how passionate people were about inclusion."
Headteacher, Team Building Event, 2009

Teams can develop images of the future we want to create together, along with the values that will be important in achieving this and the goals they want to see attained along the way. Unfortunately, many people still think vision is the top leader's job. In schools, children's centres and other settings, the vision task usually falls to the manager, head teacher and/or the governors, or it comes in a glossy document from the local authority or the government. However visions based on authority are not sustainable.

Drawing on the planning tools MAPS and PATH (Pearpoint, Forest and O'Brien 1997) and other facilitation sources, we use both process and graphic facilitation to enable groups to build *their* picture of what they would love to see happening within their organisation/community in the future and we encourage this to be a positive naming, not just a list of the things they want to avoid.

"So nice to reflect and realise what a long way we have come"
Children Centre Manager, Visioning day, 2010

When working with teams to create a shared vision we have found it is always worth beginning the session with a range of activities and reflections designed to set the tone for the work to be done. This needs following up with a session lasting at least an hour where all present reflect on what matters most to them about their work. This reflection should include what they would most wish to see happening if there were no constraints on time, people, resources or other factors. Individuals in twos and threes can then be asked to share their thinking first with each other then with the whole group. Participants can be encouraged to use their imaginations to the fullest and to stretch their thinking as far as they can as they describe what they would love to see happening in the future, even if they have no idea of how they could get there. This part of the process is not about being realistic; it is about establishing *the direction of travel.*

As people give voice to their thinking the essence of what they say can be captured on a large and colourful graphic mounted at the front of a room, similar to the image at the start of this section. Someone who has learned graphic facilitation skills best does the capturing of words and images.

Person Centred Planning

Typically facilitators can use person centred planning tools such as MAP and PATH to create vision and to go to do further planning with any team usefully going through a number of the following stages:

The Story So Far. This is a valuable activity for new or reorganised teams where trust levels may not be high; this activity can last for up to an hour and asks team members to describe their professional journeys so far, the high and low points and the key changes. The end graphic poster typically captures the complexity of the past and the ever-changing territory the team works within. For some teams this process is key to allowing them to take the step into the future that building a shared vision requires. There can be a therapeutic value in naming the past, literally drawing a line around it and moving on.

- *Headline Themes.* This is a 15 to 20 minute activity, which asks the group to capture the essence of their vision in 3 or 4 memorable headline-type summary phrases.

- *Naming the Nightmare.* No more than 5 to 10 minutes is needed for this activity. Here we ask people to name their nightmares, the things they would hate to see happening in their organisation or community. We don't dwell on this nor do we encourage the same level of detailed description that we expect in the vision. However we have learned that some teams/individuals need the extra energy that is released by naming and working to avoid the nightmare.

- *A Year from Now.* A 30 to 45 minute activity which asks the team to imagine they have traveled in time and are now a year ahead from today and are looking back at what they have achieved. The rule is that the events they remember must be both positive and possible. This is a more playful activity and often releases energy and creativity in the team

- *Naming Roadblocks and Barriers.* This is a 45-minute activity which asks the team to name what they see as the significant barriers standing in the way of achieving their vision. We encourage the group to be as specific as they can about these

roadblocks as they write them onto cards, which are then posted over the vision graphic. The team then problem solves together in twos and threes devising ways of going round, removing or reducing the roadblocks until a point is reached where most of the vision is uncovered again. This is an energising activity for teams that feel overwhelmed by the sheer number of issues confronting them.

- *Who do we need to take with us on the Journey towards the Vision.* This is a 20 minute activity that asks the team to name key people who will need to be fully on board before work on the vision can begin in earnest. This activity begins with the people in the room who are invited to sign up to the vision there and then. The team is also asked to create a (small) list of supporters with whom the vision should be shared. With the creation of this list the team begin to chart some their first actions from the day – who will enroll who?

- *Who are we? Gifts, Strengths and Talents.* This is a 30 minute activity which encourages the team to take explicit stock of their capacities and what they already have going for them as they begin working towards the vision. We do this in various ways such as asking individuals to talk about a time in their professional lives (or beyond) when they felt they were at their best and by asking the group as a whole to notice and name each others gifts and talents. This is a strong reminder to teams of the wealth of knowledge and experience that is already and always in the room.

- *Charting Specific Actions.* This is a 30 to 40 minute activity done initially in pairs and then in groups of four. The team members are asking to start naming a sample of actions they can do in the next few days/week/month and how these actions relate to the vision. We actively coach the group to name actions that they themselves are going to do (not simply a good idea for someone else to do) and which are more than just good intentions.

These ideas and way of working have emerged from the work of Jack Pearpoint, Marsha Forest, John O'Brien and the people across the world inspired by them plus our own unpublished experiences of facilitating many teams across the UK. They are processes designed to promote and support the inclusion of individuals in the

mainstream world and so fit very well with teams working for inclusion.

These visioning and planning processes work best with external facilitation but even without this, the creation of a shared articulated vision with a plan that supports the direction of the dream would be essential for any inclusive team.

"Our plans miscarry if they have no aim. When a man does not know what harbour he is making for, no wind is the right wind."
Seneca

Community and Teams

Who will you need to take with you? This is a crucial stage. Who are the key stakeholders in the change towards a more inclusive team? How can you best enrol their support? What about the wider community in which your team operates?

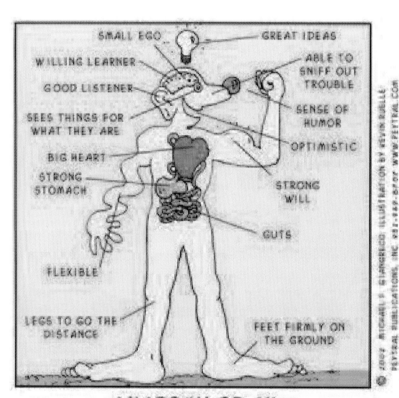

ANATOMY OF AN
EFFECTIVE TEAM MEMBER

"People only support what they create. Life insists on its freedom to participate and can never be coerced into accepting someone else's plans"
Wheately, 2005.

Wheatley (2005) argues that we should abandon mechanistic assumptions about organisational change as **meaning behaves more like energy**. Following this logic we do not have to achieve a critical mass, or roll out programmes across a whole setting or community. Instead we can work locally finding creative ideas that are meaningful to one area of the team or system. Energy generated here will lead to other networks taking notice. Inkblots are dropped and spread...

Wheatley (2005) argues strongly for engaging participation processes when undergoing change. She states we should involve everybody who cares and anyone likely to be affected by changes:

> **"We haven't yet absorbed the simple truth that we can't force anybody to change. We can only involve them in the change process from the beginning and see what's possible. If change becomes meaningful to them, they will change. If we want their support, we must welcome them as co-creators."**

In 2006, we at *Inclusive Solutions* were involved in a consultation with the communities of all the emerging children's centres in Oxfordshire. Oxfordshire was keen that local residents and parents' ideas and vision for the future inform them on how their teams of the future should 'feel'.

Many thought that the children's centre should be a focus for community building and connection: this was a strongly recurring theme in all of the sessions we conducted. In some visions this was expressed as the creation of a co-operative community, a village of support where the gifts of all were recognised and used, as one participant said: "a place where we can learn what each has to give". In other visions there was a wish for the aims and activities of the centre to be owned and driven by local people. In yet others the centre was a place to gather for mutual support and friendship. The essence of the aspiration being expressed here was to take charge of the future for the community's children.

Building on the last chapter we see that the available literature on community building (e.g. Kretzmann and McKnight 1993) strongly suggests that communities cannot be built (or rebuilt) by focusing on their needs, problems and deficiencies. Rather, community building starts with the process of locating assets, skills and capacities of residents, local associations and institutions. The vision being expressed here is radically different from the approach that begins with identifying the problems and needs within a

community and it is worth rehearsing some of the drawbacks of a needs-driven approach to problem solving and community building.

Viewing a community as an endless list of problems and needs leads directly to the much-criticised fragmentation of services and efforts to provide solutions and thus provokes the subsequent calls for a one-stop shop of services. It also denies the basic community wisdom (expressed throughout the visions described here) which realises problems are tightly interconnected and in fact symptomatic of the breakdown of a community's own problem solving capacities.

Targeting resources based on needs directs funding not to residents but to service providers, a consequence not always planned for or effective. Making resources available on the basis of needs can have negative effects on the nature of local community leadership. If, for example, a measure of effective leadership is the ability to attract resources, then local leaders/centre managers are in effect, being forced to devalue their families and their communities by highlighting their problems and needs and by ignoring their capacities and strengths.

Providing resources on the basis of needs underlines the perception that only outside experts can provide real help. Therefore the relationships that count most for local residents are no longer those inside the community, those neighbour-to-neighbour links and informal supports much mentioned in these consultations. Instead the most important relationships become those that involve the expert, the social worker, the health provider and the funder. Once again the relationships that bind communities together are weakened.

At best reliance on identifying and meeting needs as the sole policy guide will only ensure a maintenance and survival strategy targeted at isolated individual clients, not a development plan that can involve the energies of an entire community.

So if we accept that trying to address the big issues facing children's centres and other teams concerned with the education, care and socialisation of children, will not be achieved by simply increasing services, what else is needed?

One of the best researched answers to this question that we are aware of is detailed within Lisbeth Schorr's book: *Common Purpose – Strengthening Families and Neighborhoods to Rebuild America.* She

lists what she terms the 'Seven Attributes of Highly Effective Programs' as follows:

1. Successful programs are comprehensive, flexible responsive and persevering
2. Successful programs see children within the context of their families
3. Successful programs deal with families as parts of neighbourhoods and communities
4. Successful programs have a long-term, preventative orientation, a clear mission and continue to evolve over time
5. Successful programs are well managed by competent individuals with clearly identifiable skills
6. Staffs of successful programs are trained and supported to provide high-quality, responsive services
7. Successful programs operate in settings that encourage practitioners to build strong relationships based on mutual trust and respect.

Community Circles

Community circles were mentioned in the earlier chapter on the intentional building of relationships. Unsurprisingly we revisit them now when considering community. In 2007 we at *Inclusive Solutions* began to create community gatherings in Nottinghamshire that were based on full inclusion principles. All were welcome to explore how all could get sufficient meaning, friendship and money in their lives.

> "The deepest dream of ABCD is that more and more people can come to see truly that 'there is no one we don't need' and that a community without a place for everyone is a community really with a place for no one."
>
> --Mike Green

Our own community building work was inspired by the highly successful work of *Beyond Welfare* in Iowa, in the United States. In response to poverty, allies and participants were gathered and their wants, needs and offers shared.

This kind of community enlisting seems to fit well with the work of Kretzmann and McKnight (1993), Wheatley (1995) as well as that encouraged by Mike Green and others involved in what has become known as *Asset Based Community Development*. (2007)

"This process welcomes participants into community, assists them in identifying their strengths as well as challenges, and introduces them to the values of relationship, reciprocity and leadership development that infuse everything that BW does. Allies are also recruited, trained and supported for intentional friendships with BW participants that are based on common interests. The safety and stability, self-sufficiency, and well-being of the BW participant family remains at the center of these relationships. BW assists families that are particularly isolated in enlisting a Circle of Support, a group of 3-4 volunteers that meets monthly to understand and support the goals of the family."
Hidden Treasures: Community Building Workbook,

It is interesting to note the linkage between the theme of community engagement in change and the *Head Teacher Standards* and *Standard 6: Strengthening Community* in particular, which would be just as relevant to the work of managers of early years settings:

"Schools exist in a distinctive social context, which has a direct impact on what happens inside the school. School **leadership** should commit to engaging with the internal and external school **community** to secure equity and entitlement. Head teachers should collaborate with other schools in order to share expertise and bring positive benefit to their own and other schools. They should work collaboratively at both strategic and operational levels with parents and carers and across multiple agencies for the well-being of all children. Head teachers share responsibility for **leadership** of the wider educational system and should be aware that school improvement and **community** development are interdependent."
Head Teacher Standard 6, Strengthening Community 2006.

So the opening up of participation, community engagement and cohesion processes is essential. Focusing on capacity with maximal and inclusive involvement beyond the team members themselves, is crucial to building a team that shares a vision of full inclusion.

If enough quality groundwork has been done in the first three steps of the medicine wheel, then the management stage should almost be starting to shape itself. With the foundations of leadership, vision and community in place, the team is ready to get into action and it will then grow and develop its own momentum.

- So who is going to do what and when?
- What does the action plan look like?
- What resources will be needed?
- Where will this work take place and when?
- Where will this work be named in the Development or Improvement Plan?

Teams in Action: Harnessing the Diversity of a Team

Teams need a range of gifts and strengths to be effective. They need a range of styles of thinking and acting if they are to avoid becoming stuck or ineffective when it comes to including children and young people with a wide range of difference and challenges.

In Howard Gardner's latest book *Five Kinds of Minds (2007)* we can usefully reflect on the distinctive thinking styles available to any group of individuals. Edward De Bono had previously provided many helpful, guiding ideas around ways of thinking with his *6 Thinking Hats*. We believe it is useful to consider how each hat reflects a different style of thinking for someone in an inclusive team or elsewhere. These are explained below:

Red Hat
Wearing the red hat, you look at problems using intuition, gut reaction, and emotion. You try to think how other people will react emotionally and articulate your own feelings – positive and negative.

White Hat
With this thinking hat you focus on the data available. Look at the information you have, and see what you can learn from it. Look for gaps in your knowledge, and either try to fill them or take account

of them. With this hat you analyse past trends, and try to extrapolate from historical data.

Grey Hat

Using grey hat thinking, you look at all the negative possibilities of the decision or your team situation. You look at it cautiously and defensively. You try to see why it might not work. This hat is important because it highlights the weak points in any team plan or endeavour. It allows you to tackle weaknesses, alter them, or prepare contingency plans to counter them. Grey hat thinking helps to make your plans tougher and more resilient. It can also help you to spot fatal flaws and risks before you embark on a course of action. Grey hat thinking can be very useful, as many successful people get so used to thinking positively that often they cannot see problems in advance. This leaves them under-prepared for difficulties.

Yellow Hat

The yellow hat helps you to think positively. It is the optimistic viewpoint that helps you to see all the benefits of the decision and the value in it. Yellow hat thinking helps you to keep going when everything looks gloomy and difficult.

Green Hat

The green hat stands for creativity. This is where you can develop creative solutions to a problem. It is a freewheeling way of thinking, in which there is little criticism of ideas – your 'internal censor' is switched of as you search for the seeds of real possibility within what might seem a hopelessly impractical idea

Blue Hat

The blue hat stands for leadership and vision. This is the hat worn by people chairing meetings or leading in teams. The blue hat wearer listens to the perspectives of all the other hats and looks to the future. When running into difficulties because ideas are running dry, they may direct activity into green hat thinking. When contingency plans are needed, they will ask for grey hat thinking, and so forth.

We propose an extra hat:

The Values Hat

You wear this hat to name the deeper values that underpin your work in a team for inclusion; to remind each other why you do this work in the first place - because, for example: 'this child has a human right to belong!' Human rights, equality, an end to

Inclusive
Solutions

discrimination and segregation – the voicing of the values hat serves to put the team back on track around what matters most to them at those times when they may have gotten lost in the details or distracted by petty frustrations.

No one hat is better or more important than another in this activity. Each has its own distinctive take on the issues the team is trying to move forward on. Whilst this activity is playful on the surface it is proven in helping teams act more creatively, in interrupting habitual ways of thinking and letting a fresh set of ideas emerge.

The more diverse the team the richer and more inclusive it can become. This is very evident when problem solving engages a wider group of team members than usual. We have noticed many times how the involvement of a setting's secretary/admin person or their site manager has enhanced solutions and strategies to stuck issues.

GUARDIAN ANGEL   SUPER-MAGNET

STUCK LIKE GLUE   HOVERCRAFT

HELPING OR HOVERING?

Teams committed to effective inclusion will need to be great at problem solving together. They will need to be positive and solution-oriented but will also need to be able to contain and process more painful and hard to resolve issues and emotions too. In some situations bearing witness, trying to restore hope, or just hanging in there through a very difficult time may be the most respectful responses to a child and a family's circumstances.

Teams Problem Solving Together

However in a myriad of other circumstances the instinct to get creative around hard to solve issues needs structured processes. One such tool is *The Solution Circle*. Solution circles can be used for

quick problem solving around stuck issues and can be very powerful for all involved.

Rufford Infant School in Nottingham have a long standing commitment to inclusion and know the value of creative problem solving as a staff team with parents directly involved. The ideas and solutions named have come out of creatively thinking outside the box, teamwork and experimentation.

"**Finding a way of calming children who have severe autism is always a challenge - but find it we must if they are to make personal and academic progress. With James it was always having a toy model of Captain Scarlett near by. When angry and tipping chairs over or throwing anything that came to hand, giving him the model of Captain Scarlett calmed him immediately.**

Marana had severe autism but with severe learning difficulties too. Enabling her to be part of the class group was a great challenge because she couldn't engage with anyone. But we found a way to enable her to remain in her class without screaming or even the hall at service times. By chance we found she liked listening to Bob Marley. So throughout her small and large group times Bob Marley would be playing quietly in the background and this enabled her to be calm through planned activities. When she left us she took a CD of Bob Marley with her.

Parandeep was different again. She was a spinner. We found that she liked duplicates of all small toys - toys that she could hold, one in each hand. We purchased a wide range of small duplicate toys so that when she screamed and became very agitated we could provide her with them. With one in each hand she would spin them in opposite directions - a skill no staff member managed to master. She calmed and flapped and smiled and then she was back on course to do some work."

Jude Berry, Headteacher, Rufford Infant School, Nottingham, 2009.

Inclusive
Solutions

Solution Circle: A Fast Problem Solving Tool

Solutions Circles use both Graphic and Process Facilitation that enables teams and individuals to get 'unstuck' from a problem where they likely feel they have 'tried everything'. 'Solution Circles' were developed by Jack Pearpoint and Marsha (1996)

For a full description of the Solution Circle process see:
http://www.inclusion.com/ttsolutioncircle.html

Solution Circle Method

A Solution Circle has 4 discrete steps, each of roughly equal length and can be facilitated in as little as 20 minutes. 2 facilitators are needed to run the Circle; one to time-keep and manage the process, the other to create a graphic record of each step.

Step 1: PRESENT PROBLEM: The problem presenter is invited to describe for the wider listening group everything they think the group needs to know about the stuck situation – what's been tried so far with what result. It is worth reassuring the problem presenter that they do not necessarily make sense or even tell a coherent story at this point – tell them it it is OK to ramble! It is also OK for the problem presenter to sit silently for a time – there is no pressure on them to fill every second of the time available. During this first step the wider group stays silent – there is no opportunity to ask questions or seek clarification from the problem presenter

Step 2: CREATIVE TEAM: The listening group now has their turn, the problem presenter remains silent throughout Step 2. The process facilitator invites a quick fire round of potential solutions and ways forward in dealing with the stuck situation they have just heard about. Short, snappy, in-a nutshell solutions are what's needed in this step – no long analyses or complex theories – there isn't time – the group will be going their separate ways in 10 or 15 minutes and there are 4 steps to compete!

Step 3: DIALOGUE: Asks the problem presenter to choose a couple of the ideas generated by the team that they would like to hear a bit more about. Step 3 develops 2 or 3 solutions and there is time for some short focussed dialogue between the problem presenter and the wider team. There is not time for the problem presenter to say why certain solutions suggested in Step 2 would not work. The facilitators must keep the group concentrating on moving forward

Step 4: NEXT STEPS: Group and problem presenter figure out together one or two actions they will take within the next day or two. Facilitators need to ensure these are grounded actions and not 'good intentions'. To reinforce this someone form the wider group is asked to volunteer to act as a 'coach' to the problem presenter and give them a call in a week or so to ask how they got on with the first steps

End the Solution Circle with a round of reflections from each participant on the session they have just had together and finally the graphic facilitator gives the completed graphic to the problem presenter.

Circle of Adults

Circle of Adults (Newton and Wilson, 2006) is a lengthier but deeper approach to team reflection and problem solving.

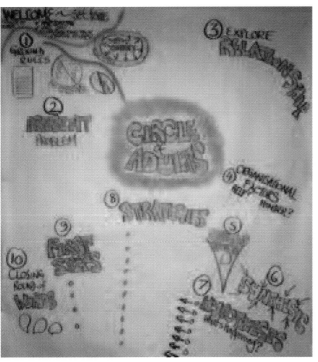

Again we believe that the more complex the problem, the more diverse the team needs to be; this is vital if understanding and relationships with challenging young people are to be at their best. We developed this approach in the face of intractable behaviour problems in schools, a rising tide of exclusions. It is also a response to a disturbing, instinctive attitude that a high number of pupils 'just don't belong here'.

Building on earlier attempts to develop group supervision, teamwork and mutual support among teachers (as laid out by Hawkins and Shohet,1989 and Hanko, 1990, 1999) this model has

evolved to become a robust framework for exploration of the hardest to understand situations with a diverse group.

Regular meetings are held between a concerned circle of adults and as diverse a group as possible. In these groups emotions are shared, personal feelings and reactions explored as well as deeper understandings gained about individual young people and what they bring. Aspects of the system, which help and hinder are explored, and detailed problem solving is engaged in. The process culminates in shared theories and practical strategies. These groups are powerful and **do** make a difference. We feel that the task facing teachers and other professional carers and educators of understanding and coping with emotional turmoil and hard to manage behaviour is not an easy one and processes, which can offer front line staff essential group support and supervision, must be welcomed.

A Step by Step Guide to Circle of Adults

1. Group members are welcomed: theoretical values and background to the approach are outlined emphasising the importance of inclusive educational opportunities for those with most challenging behaviour and the need for team support and reflection opportunities for front line staff.

2. Introductions are made and ground rules and aims are clarified.

3. Live issues are gathered from the group: one situation of concern is selected that appears to reflect shared issues.

4. Case presentation: The teacher/worker who raised the concern is asked questions to elicit the child's 'story'. Key themes are recorded on a large graphic posted where all can see it and take note of the emerging 'big picture'. The teacher is asked to keep a clear focus on the child and is guided so as not to let their own 'ideological editor' allow judgmental thinking or inaccurate generalisations. Positives and negatives about their behaviour are elicited. Feelings are probed - 'what does it feel like being with this child?

5. One member of the group is asked to actively listen to the presentation and subsequent discussions from the perspective of

the young person him/herself.

From time to the process facilitator asks this member of the group how they are feeling about what they have heard so far.

6. Additional questions/information from the group about pupil are gathered from those present

7. The process of relationship is described: the story of the teacher's relationship with the young person is described. Metaphors and analogies are invited. How would a fly on the wall see your relationship? If you were alone together on a desert island, what would it be like?

8. Impact of previous relationships/spillage from one relationship to another (transference/emotional resources explored): teachers are asked who or what situation they are reminded of? They are asked whether there has been any transfer of past relationships onto the child or projection of their feelings into the child? For instance, does this situation remind you of any of those angry but helpless feelings you had with your own son when he was and adolescent? Exploring the child's possible transference, questions are posed such as, is any role being transferred onto teachers by the child? For instance, are you being treated as if you were her father?

9. Counter transference: what feelings actions or thoughts are being used to counter this transference from child to the teacher? For instance, are you doing anything to avoid being treated as if you were his parent?

10. System/Organisational factors: what aspects of the school's organisation help or hinder this pupil's emotional/behaviour development? What areas of the curriculum provide successful experiences for the child? For instance does the pastoral system of the school provide space, or time and skilled personnel able to counsel this young person and work actively with their parents?

11. Synthesis of emerging themes by the graphic facilitator. The content of the graphic so far is summarised and the group's attention is drawn to emerging themes.

12. What understandings/hypotheses can we begin to draw out

from the emerging story? This is an important stage and it is essential to keep thinking rich and open ended, inviting as many as possible hypotheses. Participants need to be led through a creative brainstorm of understandings, and theories that might begin to explain what is happening.

13. What alternative strategies/interventions are open to be used? These need to be brainstormed and recorded.

Either/ors need to be avoided at this time also. This needs to be a shared session in which the teacher who is presenting the concern contributes as much as anyone. Care is needed to ensure that this person is not overloaded with other people's strategies. The problem presenter has final say on strategy selection.

14. First steps agreed. Presenter of the issue then selects the next steps they will pursue and with what strategies. Where possible a coach is appointed to check in with the problem presenter that agreed deadlines for completion of first steps are met.

A team can become much more inclusive in its operations both within and without. Teams can commit to the full inclusion of all children and young people. Leaders can set this out as the new direction, create a sense of shared vision and work hard to take people with them both within and outside the organisation. Ultimately there will be a day-to-day management task and some shared figuring out of how every person will be included. We now know that this can be achieved.

"Ghandi was reversing the materialistic concept that conditions determine psychology. No, psychology could shape conditions. What you think, you become."
The Life of Mahatma Gandhi, Louis Fischer, 1982.

We have explored here how a team can change with leadership, shared vision, community engagement and effective and creative management. Ultimately team leaders and team members, using the wisdom and patience of Ghandi need to live the change they wish to see.

Practical Implications

- Consider who needs a team in your personal or professional life? A child or young person? Is it a parent? Is it a practitioner? A manager? Or is it you?

- Build a diverse team. Ensure that the person inviting people to join the team is not the focus of the team.

- Choose your problem-solving tool

- Create a shared vision and begin the work

Hard Questions

- Where do you recruit a team around someone who is totally isolated and invisible to the wider world?

- How to deal positively and inclusively with those who would wish to sabotage and destroy your team

- What do you do when a *divorce* or serious irreconcilable conflict occurs between key team members?

Resources

- Newton, C. and Wilson, D., Circles of Adults, Inclusive Solutions, 2006

- Green, M., Moore, H., O'Brien, J. (2007) *When People care enough to act* Inclusion Press

- www.inclusionpress.com

Conclusion

So these are the keys to inclusion: can you use them? What doors will you open? Which children and adults can you make sure enter the mainstream world of school, college and community life? What small step can you take as a result of reading this book and your own resolve? Do something now.

Join us in our dream for full inclusion of all children and adults in our mainstream schools, settings and communities. Let us make sure all the resources that are currently diverted into special settings, special schools and units are placed at the front line of mainstream inclusion: the classroom, the workplace, the community settings.

The time is right. Let us just get on with it.

But we know there will be resistance; there always has been. Let us reflect on what will stop you doing anything differently or those you work with.

The Gargoyles of Change

"Gargoyle, **n. a grotesque carved face or figure, especially as a gutter-spout carrying water clear of a wall."**
Oxford English Dictionary

Inspired by the work of Inclusion Press as so much of our work has been, Jack and Marsha's idea of 'the monsters of change' and with a little medieval European church architecture mixed in, let us consider the Gargoyles of Change!

Many forces and issues internal and external to us all can prevent change, especially when the change in question is greater inclusion of children and adults who have not typically attended mainstream schools and settings.

Fear, control and *complacency* are the most powerful gargoyles and each regularly stop us all from moving forward radically or more quickly in the direction of a fully inclusive world featuring mainstream schools with no reliance on special schools or units.

Gargoyles as created on many ancient churches across the world but strikingly in parts of the UK and wider Europe represent the very essence of keeping evil spirits at bay. They often spurt water, are made of stone and were made particularly frightening to ward off evil spirits.

Not unlike the purveyors of negative attitudes they can spout at great length, can appear to be immoveable and rock-like and have facial expressions to send the most optimistic change seekers scurrying for cover!

We have learned to love gargoyles for their fascinating diversity, history and many charms. When we invite people to dramatically portray gargoyles there is not much room for ambiguity.

When a grotesque is created to demonstrate fear it is very clear what we are looking at!

When training, we invite three participants to create each of the three gargoyles with their bodies and facial expressions. We ask them to express the very essence of the following three obstacles to change... (This is a deliberately 'over the top' and light-hearted activity, using humour allows us to name worst case scenarios that would not be easily faced in the context of a serious discussion).

Fear   Control   Complacency

Participants dramatically depict each gargoyle, best presented in squatting, standing or lying down body positions, and we then sometimes project onto a screen one of the images above to further clarify what we are talking about!

We then open up the question to the rest of the participants: what are your worst fears? What issues of control are getting in the way of change? Who is being complacent? When general statements are made we then press for details and specifics of participant's worst fears, control issues or complacent thoughts (For example: what exactly are you afraid of?).

We invite you now as the reader of this book to face your own gargoyles of fear, control and complacency. What will hold you back? Recognise the gargoyles in yourself and then it is much easier

to recognise them in others. Have a real good look and write down in detail, or talk through exactly what issues in yourself you will have to face if you wish to take the ideas in this book further.

Once the gargoyles are out in the open and brought down to eye level they are not anywhere near as scary! Stone begins to crumble, evil spirits slip away....change can take place!

We like to point out that the gargoyles are not bad in themselves. Without their presence in our optimism might well lead to some foolish decision-making, as we all fly off the cliff singing ' happy day'.

Champions of Change

When working with groups at this stage we introduce the champions of change. The friends of change are the complete opposite of the gargoyles. These forces will make change much more likely to happen. It is not hard to evoke the champions; they are present in any group of people. They include the following:

- Vision
- Team work
- Sense of humour
- Dedication
- Persistence
- Strong values
- Optimism
- Stories that inspire and the storytellers
- Strength

The list is endless. We invite individuals to stand up as they name a champion of change and to the music of *We are the Champions* by Queen; the group sings along and sways to and fro with hands in the air. We have done this in England, Scotland, Wales, Ireland, United States, Greece and Holland.

So consider yourself and your own personal champions of change. How will you stay strong? How will you take on the gargoyles in yourself and others? What champions do you know that you can link up with? Recognise the forces within yourself that will make change much more likely to happen. But don't do it alone. Remember the Scuba Divers Law: Never Dive Alone!

Practical Implications

Work with one other person to clarify your own gargoyles and champions.

- Set up a session at the end of a training day with a group of people and bring the gargoyles to life as well as the champions.

Hard Questions

- What will you do if you are completely dominated by one of the gargoyles and just cannot free yourself?
- What if no champions appear to be present in your situation? Where can you begin?

Afterword by Maresa MacKeith

There is no doubt that we all belong together. To get to a place where resources are prioritised to make this happen is the purpose of this book.

Our society, in Britain, with its history of segregation and exclusion has powerful forces to maintain the belief that some people do not belong in the mainstream of life. We need the vision and planning tools of this book if those forces are going to be diverted to enable us all to get to know each other as peers and equals. Our society will only grow if we learn to appreciate what those, often taken away from the mainstream, have to give.

My experience of being separated from the mainstream world still haunts me. The viciousness, of not having my value as a person recognised or having the opportunity to learn as I wanted to, is something I don't want to be inflicted on anybody else. Yet I still see that violence every day in the name of giving people what they need in a special place. It is not a kindness to separate. I think it has to be understood as a violation of our humanity and ability to connect.

We are all different and the line between being seen as a valued human being or not is variable. The history of the 'other' race, religion, appearance or ability, we have all seen as one of condescension or violence. Our security as people rests on knowing we will be wanted by those around us whatever happens to us.

References and Other Resources

Arbib, M. A., Billard, A. Lacoboni, M. and Oztop, E. (2000), *Synthetic Brain Imaging: Grasping, Mirror Neurons and Imitation* Elsevier Science Ltd

Asset Based Community Development Institute (2005). *Hidden Treasures. Community Building Workbook*

Audit Commission, (2002). *Special Educational Needs: a Mainstream Issue,*

'Beyond Welfare' and other asset-based community building initiatives in North America go to:
www.sesp.northwestern.edu/docs/abcd/hiddentreasures.pdf

Block, P. (2008). *Community: The Structure of Belonging* Berrett-Koehler Publishers, San Francisco.

Community Circles: For more on our work with community circles go to:
www.inclusive-solutions.com/communitycircles.asp

Croch, W,R. (2010). www.personality-and-aptitude-career-tests.com/culture-fair-iq-test.html

De Bono, Edward (1985). *Six Thinking Hats*

Derry, Sharon J. (ed) (1990). *Learning Strategies for Acquiring Useful Knowledge in Dimensions of Thinking and Cognitive Instruction* Hillsdale, New Jersey, USA.

DFES (2006). Head Teacher Standard 6: Strengthening Community in: *Head Teacher Standards*

Dixon, B. (1991). *My Dream IEP Meeting Innovations* Institute on Disability, University of New Hampshire.

Donnellan, Anne. M., and Leary, Martha R. (2009)
www.autcom.org/articles%5CMovement.html

Donnellan, A. M. and Leary, M. R. (1995). *Movement Differences and Diversity in Autism/Mental Retardation: Appreciating and Accommodating People with Communication Challenges* Wisconsin, DRI Press, Madison.

Drewery, W. (2008) Afterword in Newton, C. and Mahaffey, H. *Restorative Solutions* UK, Inclusive Solutions Limited.

Dowling, E. and Osbourne, E. (eds.) (1985) *The Family and the School: A Joint Systems Approach to Problems with Children* London, Routledge & Kegan Paul

Drewery, W. Winslade J. and McMenamin, D. (2002). *Restorative Practices for Schools* Hamilton, New Zealand, University of Waikato.

Drewery, W. (2005). Why We Should Watch What We Say: Position Calls, Everyday Speech and the Production of Relational Subjectivity in *Theory and Psychology.* 15 (3) p. 305-324.

Drewery, W. (2004). Conferencing in Schools: Punishment, Restorative Justice, and the Productive Importance of the Process of Conversation in *Journal of Community and Applied Social Psychology.* 14, p. 1-13.

Drewery, W., Winslade, J. and McMenamin, D. (2002). *Restorative Practices for Schools: Unpublished Report on Northland Project* Hamilton, New Zealand, University of Waikato.

Etmanski, A. (2002). *A Good Life* available at www.agoodlife.org

Field, T., Miller J. and Field, T. (1994). How Well Pre-school Children Know Their Friends in *Early Development and Child Care* Vol. 100 p. 101-109.

Feldman, J. (1997) *Wonderful Rooms Where Children Can Bloom* Peterborough, New Hampshire, Crystal Springs Books. (Contains over 500 innovative ideas for creating school environments where children can feel welcome, secure and nurtured)

Fischer,L. (1982). *The Life of Mahatma Gandhi,*London: Grafton Books.

Gallannaugh, Frances and Dyson, Alan (2008). Disproportionality in Special Needs Education in England in *The Journal of Special Education,* Vol. 42 (1) p. 36-46 DOI: 10.1177/0022466907313607 University of Manchester

Galton, Francis. (1883). *Inquiries into Human Faculty and Its Development.* First Edition, Macmillan.

Gardner, Howard (1983). *Frames of Mind: The Theory of Multiple Intelligences.* New York (publisher here).

Prof. Dr. Hans-Hilger Ropers and Prof. Dr. Randolf Menzel (2007). Basic Intelligence Quotient cited at: www.diss.fu-berlin.de/diss/receive/FUDISS_thesis_000000002860?lang=en in Search for Genes Involved in Human Cognition

Grow. Gerald, (1994, 1996). *Serving the Strategic Reader: Cognitive Reading Theory and its Implications for the Teaching of Writing.* Unpublished.

Giangreco, M. et al, (1998). *Choosing Options and Accommodations for Children: A Guide to Educational Planning for Students with Disabilities* (2nd ed.) Baltimore, Paul H. Brookes Publishing Company.

Gold, D. (1994). We Don't Call It a Circle: The Ethos of a Support Group in *Disability and Society,* 9 (4) p. 435-452.

Graef, R. (2001). *Why Restorative Justice? Repairing the Harm Caused by Crime.* London, Calouste Gulbenkian Foundation.

Giangreco, M. (2002) *Absurdities and Realities of Special Education – Cartoons by Michael Giangreco* Minnetonka, Peytral Publications

Gould, S.J. (1996) *The Mismeasure of Man* New York, W.W. Norton

Green, M., Moore, H. and O'Brien, J. (2007). *When People Care Enough to Act* Toronto, Inclusion Press.

Hall, C. and Delaney, J. (1992). How a Personal and Social Education Programme Can Promote Friendship in *The Infant Class Research in Education* 47. p. 29-39.

Hawkins, P. and Shohet, R. (1989). *Supervision in the Helping Professions* Milton Keynes, Open University Press.

Hanko, G. (1990). *Special Needs in Ordinary Classrooms* Hemel Hempstead, Simon Schuster Education.

Hanko, G. (1999). *Increasing Competence Through Collaborative Problem-Solving* London, David Fulton.

Select Committee Education and Skills Report: Special Educational Needs July 2006. HC.

Jackson, Luke (2002). *Freaks, Geeks and Asperger Syndrome: A User Guide to Adolescence* London, Jessica Kingsley

Kluth, Paula (2009). www.paulakluth.com/articles/diffstrategies.html

Kluth, P. and Schwarz, P. (2008) *Just Give Him the Whale* Baltimore, Paul Brookes (available from www.inclusive-solutions.com)

Kohler, T. and Earl, S. (2004) *"Waddie Welcome and the Beloved Community"* Inclusion Press, Toronto. (A story of community building from Savannah, Georgia. Describes the creation of relationship around a person - Mr Waddie Welcome – who was at risk of exclusion because of his impairment)

Kretzman, J. and McKnight, J. Building Communities form the Inside out ACTA publications, 1993, pp 210-223

J Leadbetter. (2005). Activity Theory as a Conceptual Framework and Analytical Tool within the Practice of Educational Psychology in *Educational and Child Psychology*, 22 (1) p. 18- 28.

PLASC and School Level Annual School Census: Pupil Level Annual School Census (PLASC), 2002-2003, Department for Education and Skills (DfES)

Leyden, G. (1978) "The Process of Reconstruction." In W.E.C. Gillham (ed.) *Reconstructing Educational Psychology.* London: Croom Helm

Lokke, C., Gersch, I. M'gadzah, H. and Frederickson, N. (1997) The Resurrection of Psychometrics: fact or fiction? Educational Psychology in Practice, 12, 4, 222-233.

MacKeith, Maresa, (2008). Who is Listening? in *Inclusion Now*, Volume 21 Autumn, 2008.

Mahaffey, H. and Newton, C. (2008). *Restorative Solutions* Inclusive Solutions

Mallory, B.L. and New, R.S. (1994). Social Constructivist Theory and Principles of Inclusion: Challenges for Early Childhood Special Education in *Journal of Special Education* Volume 28 (3) p. 322-337.

Mason, M. (2006) *Let It Be Us And other Poems* Trafford Publishing, Oxford. Order Online at: Trafford.com/o6-0031

McKnight J., (1995) *The Careless Society* Basic Books, New York

Miller, A. (1994). Parents and Difficult Behaviour: Always the Problem or Part of the Solution? in Gray, P., Miller, A. and Noakes, J. (eds) *Challenging Behaviour in Schools* London, Routledge.

Mosley, J. (1991, 1996). *Quality Circle Time in the primary classroom* Cambridge, LDA

Newton, C. and Wilson, D., (2005). *Creating Circles of Friends* United Kingdom, Inclusive Solutions.

Newton, C. and Wilson, D., (2006). *Circles of Adults* United Kingdom, Inclusive Solutions.

O'Brien J. and O'Brien C. L. (2002). *Implementing Person Centred Planning* Toronto, Inclusion Press.

O'Brien, John (2002) Great Questions and The Art of Portraiture in *Inclusion News* - http://www.inclusion.com/artportraiture.html

Oldenburg, Ray (1999). *The Great Good Place* New York, Marlowe and Company.

Owen, Harrison (1997) *Open Space Technology- A User's Guide* San Francisco, Berrett Koehler Publishers

Paley, V. (1992) *You Can't Say, You Can't Play* Cambridge, Massachusetts, Harvard University Press.

Pearpoint, J. (2002) *Hints for Graphic Facilitators'* Toronto, Inclusion Press.

Pearpoint, J., Forest, M. and Snow, J. (1993). *The Inclusion Papers: Strategies to Make Inclusion Work.* Toronto, Inclusion Press.

Pearpoint, J. Forest. (1996). Solution Circles: www.inclusion.com/ttsolutioncircle.html

Perske, R., (1988). *Circles of Friends* United Kingdom, Abingdon Press.

Piaget, J. (1937 / 1954). *La construction du réel chez l'enfant / The construction of reality in the child.* New York: Basic Books.

Pollard, C. (2008). in Mahaffey, H and Newton C. (2008). *Restorative Solutions* United Kingdom, Inclusive Solutions.

Quinton, D. (1987). The Consequences of Care: Adult Outcomes from Institutional Rearing in *Maladjustment and Therapeutic Education* Volume 5, (2) p. 18-29.

Rossetti, Z. and Tashie, C. (2006). *The Least Dangerous Assumption* University of New Hampshire, Institute on Disability http://www.iod.unh.edu

Sapon Shevin, M. (2007). *Widening the Circle* Boston, Beacon.

Schorr, Lisbeth (1997). *Common Purpose: Strengthening Families and Neighbourhoods to Rebuild America.* New York, Doubleday

Shapiro, E.S., Angello, L.M. and Eckert T.L. (2004). Has Curriculum-Based Assessment Become a Staple of School Psychology Practice? An Update and Extension of Knowledge, Use and Attitudes from 1990 to 2000 in *School Psychology Review* **Questia.com - On Line Research Forum**

Shute, Nancy (2002). Madam Montessori in *Smithsonian, 33*(6), p.70-75.

Siegel, L. S., and Metsala, E., An Alternative to the Food Processor Approach to Subtypes of Learning Disabilities in Singh, N. N. and Beale, I. L. (eds.), (1992) *Learning Disabilities: Nature, Theory, and Treatment* New York, Springler-Verlag p. 45.

Smith, C. R., (1991), *Learning Disabilities: The Interaction of Learner, Task, and Setting* Boston, Allyn and Bacon, p. 63.

Smull, Michael (2000). http://www.nwtdt.com/Archive/pcp/1dayoverview.pdf

Smull, M. and Sanderson, H. (2001) *Essential Lifestyle Planning: A Guide for Facilitators* North West Training and Development Team www.nwtdt.com

Thomas, G. and Loxley, A. (2007) *Special Education and Constructing Inclusion* United Kingdom, Open University Press.

Tinker, R. (2005). *Restorative Justice Handbook.* Nottingham City/Inclusive Solutions joint publication

Venables, K. and Farrell P. in *A Psychology for inclusive education : new directions in theory and practice* / edited by Peter Hick, Ruth Kershner and Peter Farrell (2009)

Vygotsky, L. S. (1926). Source: *Educational Psychology* . Introduced by V.V. Davydov; Translated by: Robert Silverman; Published: St. Lucie Press, Florida, 1992

Wheatley, Margaret (2005) *Finding our Way* (BK Publishers)

White, M. (1993) " Developing Self Esteem." in Bovair, K. and McLaughlin, C. (eds) *Counselling in Schools* - A Reader D. Fulton Publishers

Wien, A. (2009) www.news.bbc.co.uk/1/hi/education/4183166.stm

Wiggins, G. P., & McTighe, J. (2006). Examining the teaching life. *Educational Leadership*, March, v63 n6 p26-29

Wilson, D. (2002) *Teams for Inclusion*: Special Children

Wilson, D. 2009: Listening for a story vs. Listening to a story' (Unpublished Paper)

Inclusive
Solutions